THE
OZ FAMILY
KITCHEN

THE
OZ FAMILY
KITCHEN

more than 100 simple and delicious
real-food recipes from our home to yours

LISA OZ

HARMONY BOOKS
New York

Copyright © 2015 by Lisa Oz

Photographs copyright © 2015 by Quentin Bacon

All rights reserved.

Published in the United States by Harmony Books, an imprint of the Crown Publishing Group, a division of Penguin Random House LLC, New York.

www.crownpublishing.com

Harmony Books is a registered trademark, and the Circle colophon is a trademark of Penguin Random House LLC.

All photographs are copyright of Quentin Bacon except those photographs in which Mehmet Oz appears and the family photograph on page 12, which is courtesy of Jeff Lipsky.

Library of Congress Cataloging-in-Publication Data

Oz, Lisa.
The Oz family kitchen / Lisa Oz.—First edition.
    pages cm
Includes index.
1. Cooking. 2. Oz, Lisa—Family. I. Title.
TX714.O98 2015
641.3—dc23   2015009126

ISBN 978-1-101-90323-0
Ebook ISBN 978-1-101-90324-7

Printed in Hong Kong

Jacket design by Michael Nagin
Jacket photographs by Quentin Bacon

10 9 8 7 6 5 4 3 2 1

First Edition

CONTENTS

FOREWORD

MEHMET OZ, MD

grew up eating the Standard American Diet, often referred to by its acronym SAD (because you feel this way after consuming it). My parents had emigrated from Turkey, where the ancestral food is based on the healthy Mediterranean diet. But once in the States, they wanted to assimilate, so we copied our neighbors and focused on convenience and efficiency. We did not put a lot of thought into meals in terms of either health or pleasure.

I had never even met a vegetarian—until Lisa turned my world upside down. I tried to impress her with a home-cooked dinner for our first date. The only thing I knew how to make was chicken wrapped in aluminum foil. She thanked me for the effort but explained that she didn't eat chicken. I figured we could go out for dinner instead and took her to Pat's Cheese Steak in South Philly only to learn that she didn't eat steak either.

Despite this double faux pas, I was still invited to meet her parents at their home. Lisa was in the kitchen with her mom making a big pot of fresh tomato sauce, using vegetables from their garden while her father toiled over his specialty "gypsy" salad. Her five younger siblings were milling around, sometimes chipping in (or getting in the way). The entire experience was a celebration of life with conversations over whether the whole grain pasta was al dente or overdone. Did the herb vinaigrette need more punch? And everyone ate together, connecting (and arguing) with one another as people have done for all of human history. Meals were the familial glue for my in-laws. Even the road trips and vacations were organized around food.

They also seemed to understand that what they were eating had a profound impact on their well-being. The nutritional value of foods was a frequent topic in the home, and food that was full of empty calories or potentially toxic additives was never welcome at the table.

This is the snapshot of healthy eating that Lisa inoculated into our family when I made the wisest decision of my life and married her two years later.

In the beginning, not every meal was memorable for the right reasons. There were times Lisa's experimentation in the kitchen resulted in less than optimal results, like a curry so hot I could barely breathe. But ultimately her passion for cooking translated into a real talent for creating healthy dishes that tasted amazing.

As an intern in a busy city hospital, I quickly realized that the best meals I could eat were the ones I brought from home. I would ride my bike on the George Washington Bridge over the Hudson River with a backpack full of sandwiches in Ziploc bags and soup in Tupperware containers. In my on-call room I would eat my solitary meals and think of the love that went into their preparation. The gently toasted bread reminded me that Lisa cared, even more so the meticulously diced garlic she folded into the tunafish.

As I did my rounds on sleepy patients staring at their cardboard-like waffles or desiccated egg options at six a.m., I had a massive epiphany. I needed to change how they lived their lives, starting with their basic approach to eating, otherwise I was not fulfilling my Hippocratic obligation as a physician.

Thanks to Lisa, I respected the power of food, often commenting that when you walk into a grocery store, you are really walking into a pharmacy. But this is not a message that changes minds. People change based on what they *feel* more than what they know. To really engage change, we have to make it easy for folks to do the right thing.

After hearing me complain about the hypocrisy of taking a band-saw to people's chests to perform open-heart surgery without meaningfully impacting lifestyle changes, Lisa created our first TV show, *Second Opinion*. My first guest was Oprah and the rest is history.

Throughout the voyage, Lisa continued to feed me and our children with delicious, wholesome meals. Those dishes make up the bulk of this book. The recipes are about joyful eating that happens to be healthy—unrefined, unprocessed, real food made at home. They are designed to help you live fully, with passion, through meals that tantalize your senses while nourishing your body.

INTRODUCTION

Do you ever feel you are in a weird déjà vu loop? I do, mostly at cocktail parties. When people meet me for the first time, their reactions are almost always the same: "You're married to Dr. Oz? Oh, my gosh, what do you guys eat at home?" What I want to reply is: "Kale. Only kale." But that would be a lie.

This book is an attempt to answer the question truthfully, to give you a glimpse of what goes on in our kitchen. The recipes I've included here are the ones we actually make on a daily basis. They are designed for busy moms (and dads) who want to provide nourishing meals that the whole family will enjoy. Most of the dishes are plant-based, though some do have meat. Many are gluten free. They are generally healthful, but there are a few special-occasion treats that might surprise you. (Yes, Mehmet really does have German chocolate cake on his birthday.)

I know the thought of "America's doctor" eating cake may make some of you uncomfortable. For purists, there's no bending the rules— ever. Whether the forbidden food is meat or wheat, fat or sugar, there will always be those who feel that any deviation from the prescribed form of eating is unacceptable. Others will be elated by the idea, using it as an excuse to toss the whole "healthy food thing" out the window and go on a self-proclaimed "Oz-endorsed" binge. (Been there, done that. Very bad idea.)

So up-front apologies to anyone who thought he or she would be getting recipes for nothing but broccoli and goji berries, or super-secret diet tips to help you lose 20 pounds in 10 days. Nope, sorry. This is not that book.

It is, rather, an invitation to dine with us: to eat what we eat as a family, to share a meal and to connect over good food. And by "good" I mean both nutritious *and* delicious. Healthful food does nothing for you if you're not eating it; and if your family is anything like ours, flavorless meals are not an option, no matter how chock-full of micronutrients. For us, food is something to be enjoyed, not endured. Ideally, these dishes will both nourish the body and delight the senses. They make you healthy *and* happy.

Now, since we'll be spending some time together, allow me to introduce our clan.

We'll start with Mehmet. He's practically the poster boy for healthy eating—and that isn't always meant as a compliment. (He was once labeled a "joyless eater" after he was spied consuming his routine breakfast of Greek yogurt with blueberries.) But the truth of the matter is that Mehmet genuinely *loves* what he eats. It's just that other people don't always appreciate it. They don't understand how he can prefer carrot sticks to french fries or a bowl of quinoa to a cupcake. (However, once they taste the quinoa on page 175, it could be a different story.)

Our daughter Daphne is our resident chef. She's been cooking with me since she was old enough to balance herself on the counter, but a few years ago she graduated from culinary school. One of her favorite things is to explore new restaurants, then come home and try to replicate any outstanding menu items. She bakes when she wants to relax.

John is Daphne's husband. He likes everything (including dishes we may have accidentally burned). Just about the only thing he doesn't eat is bread, because he tries to stay gluten free as much as possible. His family is from Serbia, so he's introduced us to a whole new cuisine.

Philomena ("Philo") is their wonderful, happy toddler. She likes to hang out in the kitchen and watch us cook. At the moment, she's mostly into purées.

Our second daughter, Arabella, is generally a pescatarian, but every now and then she has a craving for "grass-fed, sustainably sourced meat." (She has occasionally been known to eat a shawarma of unknown origin on a street corner, but tends to keep that to a minimum.) She loves richly seasoned ethnic foods and makes a wicked sandwich!

Our youngest daughter, Zoe, is gluten free and dairy free. She's totally into vegetables and fruit—and, well, that's about it. (She must have gotten her taste buds from her father.) She eats seasonally, loading up on fresh melon and cherries in the summer, switching to apples and butternut squash in the fall.

Oliver, our son, is fifteen. Need I say more? Almost overnight, my sweet, little, animal-loving boy turned into a giant teenager and decided he had to eat like a *T. rex* on a rampage. Thankfully, he's willing to grill his own steaks so I don't have to get involved.

Finally, there's me. I've been a vegetarian since my early teens, with intermittent periods of being completely vegan. My mom was part of that early wave of health-conscious progressives, bucking the 1970s trend of Tang and Twinkies. She raised my siblings and me on a plant-based, whole-foods diet long before it was popular. We grew up on a farm, where we took seasonal fruits and vegetables for granted. Whether it was raspberries along the fences, apples and peaches in the orchard out back, or tomatoes fresh off the vine, there was always something ripening that we could work into our meals. I still have a weak spot for anything right out of the garden.

Okay, that's who we are in a food-related nutshell. We love to eat. And we love to cook. The kitchen is the heart of our home and the place where we spend most of our time. Everyone contributes when making the family feasts. We like to experiment—to combine tastes and textures, to incorporate ideas from places we've traveled and people we've met along the way. Our days often center on planning, preparing, and enjoying meals. We eat with enthusiasm bordering on fervor. Remember that scene in *When Harry Met Sally*? You know the one: in that scene, Meg Ryan sounds pretty much like one of us eating a bowl of perfectly cooked pasta.

While we revel in the pleasures of food, we also understand its power. We know that what we eat is a huge factor in how we feel; and for this reason, we choose food that's as close to its original form as possible. Ideally, it is whole, unrefined, GMO free, and organic. When it's available, we opt for produce that's in season and locally sourced. Processed foods are not welcome—except in very rare instances. (There are a few meat substitutes that I use sparingly when I need an umami fix.)

In spite of our shared passion, we don't always agree on what to serve. For starters, on any given weekend we have one vegetarian, two flexitarians, one pescatarian, two or three people who are eating gluten free, and a couple who may or may not be on a weight-loss plan. We also have two omnivores who will literally chow down on anything from alligator meat to fish eyeballs. Needless to say, we have a few challenges when it comes to satisfying everyone at the table.

And yet, we have made it work. We have an overarching family food philosophy that is cohesive but leaves room for diversity.

We acknowledge that no one way of eating is right for everyone. Differences in biology, geography, personality, and taste all factor into an individual's dietary choices.

I wrote this cookbook because I think there are a lot of families like ours—trying to juggle healthy options with hectic lifestyles and varied eating styles. With that in mind, I selected recipes that are full of fresh, whole-food ingredients but still easy enough to make, even on a weeknight when just getting everyone to sit down to dinner can seem daunting. I've also enlisted the help of my husband, because while his kitchen skills are basically limited to chopping and stirring, he does know how to educate people on what they need to stay healthy. Throughout these pages, you will find his advice and nutritional tips to help guide you when you make choices about what you put in your body and in the bodies of those you love.

So, welcome to our table. Please make yourself at home. We are grateful for the opportunity to spend this time together and celebrate the blessings of food and family and friendship. Now, let's eat!

—LISA OZ

TO COOK OR NOT TO COOK

I love to cook. It's a way to express my creativity, to experiment, to explore. It's also a way to show my loved ones that I care to be generous, nurturing, loving. Sometimes it even becomes meditative, in the repetitive movements of chopping and stirring. Yes, cooking can be utterly delightful.

But that's only on a good day. There's also the rest of the week—those times when there are fifty other things to do, and everyone's famished and no one wants to help get dinner on the table; and then, finally, when it's done, someone declares that he hates beets and excuses himself to get a bowl of cereal. That's when I wish I'd ordered pizza.

Yes, I totally understand that while cooking is good, it's not always easy. Mostly, it takes time and energy—two things none of us have enough of. But being organized can help maximize your use of both. For starters, try to plan what you're going to make ahead of time, especially when you're preparing meals for a large group of people. There are few things more frustrating than standing in front of an open fridge, gazing at a blur of condiments and wilting vegetables after a long day at work, while your children lurk behind you and chant in unison "What's for dinner?" It's best if you have an idea of how to answer that question before you open the refrigerator door.

Though it's not always possible, I like to start thinking about the next week's meals on Saturday or Sunday. (Usually it's on weekends that we're making a supermarket run anyway.) Before you get all nervous, please note that I just said "thinking about," not actually writing out detailed menus and making a cooking schedule (though for those of you who are super-organized, that's not a bad idea). I'm more of the "Let's get a general idea of where we're going" kind of girl.

I begin by making a smart shopping list—that means taking a brief inventory of what you've already got. (I can't tell you how many bags of brown rice I've stacked in my pantry because it's one of those things I just always pick up.) I then break the list into two categories: what we're going to eat in the next few days and what we need in the longer term. The "must eat quickly" portion includes any meats, fish, leafy greens, or berries. The things I can use all week long consist of dried goods like grains, beans, flours, and nuts, as well as some produce that includes eggs, milk, cheese, and some more "resilient" vegetables (winter squash, potatoes, cauliflower, cabbage) that will be fine sitting in the refrigerator for a few days. I make another run to the market mid-week to refresh the stock of super-perishables, but it takes a lot less time because I'm only picking up a few things.

One tip here is to eat before you go to the grocery store—and if you're taking your kids with you, make sure they've eaten, too. (Hungry children = lots of whining when you get to the cookie aisle.) If you don't have time for a meal, throw a healthy snack like nuts or an apple into your purse and munch on it in the car on the way to the market. You don't want to be lured into buying something you don't really need or want because your blood sugar is low and your resistance is even lower.

Since I mentioned the cookie aisle, I have to say up front: Stay away! Don't even walk down that aisle. There is nothing there you want in your house. Those bright colors and cleverly descriptive names are designed to entice you. And as tempting as they seem on the shelf, they are even more irresistible at 10 o'clock at night, when they're in your kitchen and your favorite TV character has just been killed off.

In general, it's best to limit your time in any of those center aisles of a supermarket. Yes, there will be things you need there, like canned goods and spices and paper plates, but it's also where most of those "nonfoods" are hanging out. One thing I do to avoid them is to shop for "the good stuff" first. I begin in the produce section and fill up my cart with fruits and vegetables. My next stop is the whole grains, dried beans, and nuts sections—items that you can often buy in bulk. By the time I've picked up the milk and eggs, or a bottle of vinegar, there's not much room left in my cart, and I'm trying to balance things in a way that won't crush the tomatoes which are now somewhere near the bottom. Finally, as I walk past an aisle with packaged, processed foods, it's like playing Jenga: one additional item and I would be heading for a shopping cart disaster.

Back at home, we do a few things to make eating healthfully easier. The first is cooking on the weekends. For me, the best thing about

this is that I have lots of hands to help. The older kids come home to visit and are great about pitching in. And the regular excuses of work (Mehmet), homework (Zoe), and sports (Oliver), which are frequently used on weekdays to get out of assisting with meals, are moot on a Sunday afternoon. Generally, everyone hangs out in the kitchen anyway, so it's easy to pass someone a knife or a colander when I'm starting to feel overwhelmed. I usually have dance music playing, so cooking together feels more like a party than actual work.

Another thing we do is double the recipe of one or two dishes so we can freeze what we don't eat and enjoy it at a later date. That way, when I'm really pressed for time, I have a whole meal I can just thaw and reheat. My favorite recipes from this book to freeze for later include the Chunky Vegetarian Chili with Quinoa (page 76), Roasted Butternut Squash Soup (page 71), Miso and Vegetable Fasting Broth (page 67), the Vegetarian Puttanesca Sauce (page 170) for pasta, Lentil and Mushroom Loaf (page 187), and Banana, Date, and Nut Muffins (page 58).

We also prepare and freeze single ingredients that may be time-consuming to fix mid-week. For example, brown rice takes a while to cook (about 45 minutes, which is an eternity when you have hungry teenagers to feed). Beans take a long time, too, both to soak and to cook (which is why on many occasions I am more than grateful for the canned versions). Cooking up big pots of beans or rice on Saturdays or Sundays when there's no rush to get dinner on the table means I'll have a quick and nutritious option at my fingertips later in the week.

We've usually got a pound or two of shrimp and a few chicken breasts tucked into the freezer, as well. These take very little time to cook, so I don't bother preparing them ahead of time, but have them available as last-minute "add-ins" to an otherwise vegetarian dish if my carnivores become feisty.

In fact, "add-ins" are the key to keeping all of our family happy at the table. You may notice that the vast majority of recipes in this book are vegetarian. That's because I believe a plant-centered diet makes the most sense for our overall physical health, as well as the health of our environment. And while other family members understand and respect this philosophy, their definition of "plant centered" is a bit broader than mine—and it includes meat, fish, or chicken several times a week. To avoid becoming a short-order cook and having to make six different entrées in order to sit down at the table, I like to start with a communal base and let everyone build his or her own plate around it.

Typically, most people's dinners start with a main-course protein and include some vegetables, and maybe a starch on the side. Though we sometimes use this model as well, I prefer to make the heart of the meal a central bowl of salad, grains, soup, or pasta—and then put out small sides of proteins (quickly sautéed chicken, shrimp, or tofu) as "add-ins" that allow everyone to customize as desired. This way I can accommodate the different dietary needs of our individuals while also enjoying a collective culinary experience.

Some of my favorite recipes for building this dinner-table model include:

Warm Quinoa and Chickpeas (page 175)
Quinoa with Mung Beans and Indian Spices (page 176)
Brown Rice Bowl with Red Curry Vegetables (page 169)
Brown Rice with Vegetable Stir-Fry and Tahini-Miso Sauce (page 166)
Fried Rice Paella with Spiced Chickpeas and Shrimp (page 178)
Mexican Chopped Salad with Creamy Chipotle Dressing (page 106)
Hijiki, Mâche, and Edamame Salad (page 113)
Salad with Peanut Dressing (page 117)
Asian Slaw with Ginger Dressing (page 119)
Oz Family Salad Bar (page 120)
"Wagababy" Pot with Udon and Asian Vegetables (page 64)
Curried Fettuccine with Roasted Squash, Chickpeas, and Hazelnuts (page 155)
Farro with Mushrooms and Thyme (page 154)
Bosphorus Breakfast with Soft-Boiled Eggs and Fruit (page 41)

Making ethnic dishes in which meat isn't the focus is a great way to cut back on the amount of animal products you eat. Our family especially loves the cuisines of India, Thailand, Turkey, and Italy. With all these cooking styles, there are so many wonderful vegetable dishes that you will barely even notice the absence of meat. Traditionally, these regional diets considered meat a luxury and it was therefore used sparingly, often just for flavoring or was reserved for celebrations and feast days.

I am often asked about foods that can help keep everyone at a healthy weight. Let me share a little secret. The best tactic is to use ingredients that look the same coming out of the ground as when you eat them. After all, the brain is not counting calories, it is counting nutrients. That's why empty calories fail to satiate us, tempting us to overeat.

—MEHMET

Speaking of celebrations, I need to mention desserts. I was toying with the idea of leaving them out of this book altogether. Truthfully, they're not recipes our family makes very often—at most, probably ten times a year, generally for birthdays or holidays. Normally, if we want something sweet after dinner, we'll grab some fruit. But sometimes we all need to mark an event with a mouth-watering indulgence. On those special occasions, we still abide by the same principles we use for everyday cooking: we use real food (in this case, milk, sugar, and butter), and we make the sweets ourselves rather than buying them "pre-fab." These are by no means health foods, but eaten sparingly they aren't too bad for you—unless, of course, you're trying to lose weight!

Some of you may be wondering about weight loss, especially since Mehmet speaks about it so frequently on his show. Frankly, most of us know what we should and shouldn't be eating when we want to drop a few pounds. The problem is almost never a matter of ignorance. (If I showed you a picture of an ice cream sundae and a piece of celery, I don't think any of you would say the ice cream is the right choice for weight loss.) The issue has way more to do with *acting* on what we already know than in uncovering some secret information.

As I mentioned in the introduction, this is not a diet book. It's a book about eating nutrient-dense, mostly plant-based foods that taste delicious. The recipes here support a healthy lifestyle, and you could use many of them in an effective dieting program but certainly not all. For anyone wondering which recipes in this book would work best on a diet, I'll just say that when I need to lose weight, the recipes I choose are things like the Banana-Blueberry Breakfast Smoothie (page 61), Miso and Vegetable Fasting Broth (page 67), and a selection of the vegetables, salads, and whole grains. I do my best to stay away from the pastas, sandwiches, and desserts.

Thankfully, our kids have always been foodies. Even when they were little, they took a genuine interest in what we were eating, and they wanted to be involved in everything from menu planning to grocery shopping to cooking. (The only thing they weren't particularly enthusiastic about was cleanup.) Though I made an effort to include all of them in the whole process, each child gravitated to a different aspect of meal preparation.

Our youngest daughter, Zoe, loved making lists. She would practice her cursive writing by carefully copying out everything I needed to buy at the market, then make a decorated menu for that evening's meal. She always liked to read it aloud and have us "order" what we wanted her to bring to the table.

Oliver was my shopping buddy. He always wanted to pick out the produce by himself, even when he was still small enough to be riding in the cart. He would make me hold open the bag for him while he dropped in the carefully chosen lemons or limes. Then he would point to a specific melon that he had to inspect before I would be allowed to place it behind him in the cart. When he was a little older, Oliver liked to be given food "assignments," during which he would leave me with the cart and run off to find the item by himself. (I made sure I could see where he was headed.)

Daphne and Arabella were both little cooks, but they approached the task very differently. Daphne was gangbusters—all in. She knew her way around the kitchen at an early age and could have taken over if I had mysteriously disappeared. Arabella was more circumspect. Rather than jump in with the washing and chopping, she preferred to hang out by the seasonings, waiting for me to stir in spices so she could taste and discover a dish as it was being born. She was always drawn to the most exotic and pungent flavors.

Even when the kids weren't cooking with me, they were in the kitchen. That's where they did their homework, colored or painted their pictures, read books, and had their excited conversations. The kitchen has always been the place where we came together as a family, but mealtimes were especially important.

We had our first two daughters while Mehmet was still a surgical resident, which meant he wasn't around a whole heck of a lot. When he did come home, it was often quite late; but we made the decision to keep the girls up so they could sit with us while we ate dinner. There were times when we thought we might be making the wrong choice (mostly on mornings when the girls were too tired to get up for school), but we felt that the time we spent together as a family ultimately would mean more than a few missed classes.

Since the children have gotten older, prioritizing these family meals has become even more significant—and difficult to arrange. With after-school activities, sports and homework, the kids' schedules are almost as hectic as ours. Often we aren't all home until after 8:00 or 9:00 p.m. But even if we don't all eat at the same time, we always make an effort to sit together, the early birds having a cup of herbal tea while the last stragglers finish their dinner.

As parents, Mehmet and I both find these moments as a family around the table to be essential. It is here that we share the events of the day and our insights into those events. *This is one of the most important ways we communicate our values to our children*, including an appreciation of the sacred nature of food and the understanding that the mundane act of sharing a meal is much more important than it seems.

WHAT WE EAT

So, what does the Oz family eat? Well, put simply, food.

Yes, I know that seems like a silly answer, but sadly it's not what many Americans are eating these days. The highly processed, colored, preserved, artificially flavored, packaged stuff that makes up a large part of the standard American diet is not food. And chances are, if you're buying something in a box (or from a drive-through window) with a long list of unpronounceable ingredients, that falls into the nonfood category.

By the way, full disclosure here: when I talk about what we eat, I mean *mostly*. While we normally make choices that are wholesome and nourishing, we have been known to answer the siren's call of salt and vinegar potato chips. The stuff that passes for food can be very appealing—even when you know better.

There are a million reasons for this. First, it's pretty darn tasty (in a highly addictive and ultimately unsatisfying way). Loaded with sugar, fat, and salt, these processed "faux foods" push our most rudimentary taste-bud buttons. Second, they are cheap (owing to subsidies and economies of scale). As an added bonus, they will last on your pantry shelf through a zombie apocalypse (thank you, preservatives and additives). And to top it all off, they are brilliantly marketed, convenient, and ubiquitous.

You may be asking: What's the big deal? If the government says something is safe for human consumption and it is being sold in a supermarket, why can't I eat it? Of course, you *can*. The odds are good that you will not keel over immediately after consuming your favorite junk food. But the drawback of these products is that they're both nutrient deficient and full of potentially harmful chemicals; and if that's what you eat on a regular basis, you are opening yourself up to a whole slew of health problems, ranging from diabetes and depression to high blood pressure and cancer. Even if you are technically disease free, eating a diet of mostly processed foods can lead to obesity, lack of energy, indigestion, bloating, brain fog, and myriad other unpleasant and uncomfortable conditions.

THE WATCH LIST

Deciding to eat healthfully is in large part a matter of figuring out what *not* to eat. And eliminating—or at least limiting—the processed products in your diet is a good place to start. With that in mind, this is a list of things we try to avoid in our home and why:

Artificial sweeteners: There is no good reason *ever* to consume this stuff. No, it won't help you lose weight. In fact, people who use artificial sweeteners actually eat more because their bodies recognize the sugary taste and go looking for the carbs that usually accompany it.

Artificial colors or flavors: These have been associated with hyperactivity in children and some cancers in rodents. Real food is beautifully colored and richly flavored, so it doesn't need these additives.

Refined foods: These foods have been stripped of their nutrients and fiber in order to prolong their shelf life and improve their texture. As a general rule, they are "the white foods"—that is, white flour, white rice, white bread, white pasta, or anything colorful that is a disguised "white food," such as cakes, cookies, cereals, and crackers. Basically, the parts that are good for you have been taken out, and you're left with nothing but empty calories.

Partially hydrogenated fats/trans fats: Found in many store-bought baked goods and fried foods, these are formed when hydrogen is added to a fat molecule to turn a liquid fat into a solid one. The new chemical structure of the fat is difficult for the body to metabolize, which leads to increased risk of cardiovascular disease.

Vegetable oils: I don't use these polyunsaturated oils (canola, soy, safflower, sunflower, cottonseed, corn, etc.) because their high omega-6 fatty acid content tends to be pro-inflammatory. Some are processed with industrial chemicals and solvents like hexane (which is a constituent of gasoline), and several are made from genetically modified crops (also an item on my "to avoid" list).

GMOs: Genetically modified organisms are plants or animals whose genome has been altered by incorporating DNA from a completely unrelated species—for example, by inserting DNA from bacteria into corn or from daffodils into rice. (I don't know about you, but that doesn't sound particularly appetizing to me.) The primary reason plants are genetically modified is to make them more compatible with industrial herbicides and pesticides.

GMOs are the subject of many lively discussions in our home. Mehmet feels that until more studies have been done, it's hard to say conclusively that they have a negative health impact. My opinion is that until more studies are done, we can't possibly assume that they are completely safe. Either way, we both agree there needs to be more independent, long-term studies on them, and we also believe that people should be able to decide for themselves whether or not to consume genetically modified foods. To do so, we need GMO labeling. Right now there's no way to know if what you're buying is GMO free unless you buy organic items or find products with the nonprofit "Non-GMO project verified" sticker on them.

In the United States, the following items are overwhelmingly genetically modified, so either I buy them organic or I don't buy them at all:

Corn products Close to 90 percent of these foods are genetically modified. (And by the way, with processed foods, you'll find corn in just about everything.) The obvious ingredient to look for is high fructose corn syrup, but that can come creeping into the

EPIGENETICS We were all taught in grade school that a baby inherits a genetic blend from his or her parents, and whatever winds up in this software code of life becomes that person's destiny. But over the past decade, a revolutionary concept called epigenetics is flipping this paradigm upside down. Our ancestors developed tools to turn our genes on or off in order to give our species the ability to rapidly adapt to a changing environment. This means we have inherited the ability to control how our genes are used.

The recipes offered in this book should support healthy epigenetic changes, although the science is too young to write an actual prescription just yet. Certainly, observations on the impact of omega-3 fats on brain development have opened everyone's eyes to the potential of this new science. And experts have even been able to measure how healthy foods can change the length of telomerase, the protein at the tips of our chromosomes that determines how we age. **—MEHMET**

food in dozens of ways, with names like maltodextrin, caramel coloring, sorbitol, dextrose, and more.

Soy products More than 90 percent of all soybeans grown in the United States are genetically modified. Much of the crop is fed to livestock but a large portion is used to make processed foods from protein shakes to meat substitutes like tofu and TVP (textured vegetable protein).

Sugar from sugar beets About 95 percent of the U.S. crop has been genetically modified, and over half our sugar is from sugar beets.

Read the label. If it doesn't say cane sugar, or organic, you can bet it's genetically modified.

Papaya About 80 percent of Hawaiian papayas are genetically modified.

Zucchini and other summer squash If you can get to a local farmers' market, buy these in season. Summer squash in January is just weird.

Processed foods If you are buying something processed or premade (cookies, crackers, soft drinks, candy, salad dressings, sauces, soups, etc.), chances are it's got some genetically modified product in it, usually in the form of corn or soy.

Non-organic meat and dairy I'm also concerned about GM alfalfa and corn in livestock feed, so that gives me one more reason (besides the overuse of hormones and antibiotics in factory farming) to buy organic meat and dairy products.

CLEAN OR DIRTY

Since I've mentioned them a couple of times already, let's talk a bit about organic foods. Ideally, we would eat only organic and avoid all herbicides, pesticides, and petroleum-based fertilizers that are part of conventional farming. But doing that can come with a hefty price tag.

Eating a predominantly clean diet can be affordable, but you need to be a discerning shopper. I'm sure you've heard of the Environmental Working Group's "Dirty Dozen" and the "Clean 15." These are lists of the best and the worst produce in terms of pesticide residue. Just so you don't have to

Google the lists, here they are (apologies to those of you who have them memorized):

THE "DIRTY DOZEN"

apples	cucumbers	potatoes
bell peppers	grapes	snap peas
celery	nectarines	spinach
cherry tomatoes	peaches	strawberries

These are the twelve fruits and vegetables you should buy organic if you don't want to be inundated with chemicals. Now, I'm not suggesting that you go crazy trying to shun them at all costs. Just do what you can, and don't stress out over it. For example, conventional spinach is way better than pretty much anything processed. But when you are shopping and you need to decide where to spend that extra money for organic produce, start here.

THE "CLEAN FIFTEEN"

asparagus	eggplants	onions
avocados	frozen sweet peas	papayas
cabbage		pineapple
cantaloupe	grapefruit	sweet corn
cauliflower	kiwis	sweet potatoes
	mangoes	

These are the fifteen fruits and vegetables that you can go ahead and buy conventional without too much concern: These either have a thick, protective skin or require fewer pesticides and therefore have a lower concentration of chemical residues than other conventional produce.

There are several types of food that we don't avoid entirely, but try to limit in our home. One of those is wheat. We love wheat-based foods (Mehmet jokes that I'm actually a carbotarian rather than a vegetarian), but they have become less and less of a staple at our meals—even the whole-grain products. Generally, we'll keep it to no more than a few meals a week. And if we have sandwiches for lunch, we won't eat pasta at dinner.

I grew up believing that whole wheat was a nourishing, high-fiber addition to a healthy diet. I'm not so sure of that now. The wheat we are eating today is not the wheat of our forefathers (or foremothers). And whether it's the hybridization or the toxic chemicals used in farming, the result is that more people seem to have problems digesting gluten (the type of protein found in wheat and similar grains).

Wheat reactions are really unpredictable. In our family, some of us are highly sensitive to it while others remain completely unaffected. The important thing is to be aware of how specific foods make *you* feel. Do certain foods give you more or less energy? Do some dishes make it harder for you to sleep at night? Do you get stomach pains after meals? Are you frequently swollen in the morning after a favorite dish? All of these could be signs of subtle food allergies.

We also keep meat to a minimum in our home. As mentioned earlier, my reasons are environmental and ethical, as well as health based. Widespread animal farming is devastating to our land quality, biodiversity, and climate. Additionally, modern farming techniques rely heavily on the use antibiotics and hormones, which make their way into our water supply. Finally, eating meat has been linked to increased incidence of chronic illnesses like cancer, heart disease, diabetes, and stroke.

I could go on and on with all the reasons it would be better for you and the planet if you gave up eating meat. But I'm not even going to try. Becoming vegetarian or vegan is a personal choice, and it's definitely not for everyone. However, the way Americans currently consume meat is unsustainable on every level. So, rather than giving up animal-based products altogether, consider *reducing* the amount you consume. Maybe you could have meat and dairy for one meal a day instead of three. Maybe just have meat on every other day. Practice "Meatless Monday" or make up your own rules for cutting back your consumption of animal products. Just a small shift in your behavior can ultimately have a huge benefit—on both a personal and a global level.

Again, I don't want you to feel that if you don't eat a completely organic, vegan, gluten-free diet, your health and the health of everyone you love, including your dog, will be ruined and you'll all end up pickled in toxic juices. Making yourself miserable because you can't live up to a near-impossible standard is silly. You do not need to be a professional chef, a nutritionist, or a camp counselor to feed your family healthful, delectable meals (though at times you may feel like all of the above). *The Oz Family Kitchen* is not about purity or perfection. It's about embracing a lifestyle that supports great health and great experiences. Just do your best to make choices that reflect your values—and have some fun while you're at it.

STOCKING UP AND GETTING READY

Now that we've discussed *what* we eat, let's talk about *how* we go about it. First, we cook. Okay, I know you're thinking that's an obvious and simplistic statement because, well, this *is* a cookbook, after all. But it's an important point. As a culture we cook less and less and we rely more and more on the food industry to make our meals for us. This has far-reaching ramifications. Obesity, chronic illness, factory farming, pollution, and the predominance of plant and animal monocultures are all effects brought about by the standard American diet of largely processed foods.

And that's all the preaching I'm going to do for today. I'm not here to make you feel guilty for giving your kid a toaster tart this morning for breakfast. I am simply stating that cooking at home with your family can have benefits way beyond the pleasure of a delicious meal.

In order to help you get organized to prepare these meals, here's a look inside our kitchen.

PANTRY
Grains

Whole grains provide the foundation for many of our meals. They are versatile and delicious, and they play very nicely with other foods, providing the perfect accompaniment for all types of beans, vegetables, and meats. They are featured in the cuisines we love the most: Italian, Thai, Indian, and Turkish. While the refined versions of some grains have been stripped of many of their nutrients, whole grains are full of vitamins, minerals, and fiber.

Brown rice: I prefer the starchy texture of short-grain brown rice, but I also use long-grain, brown basmati, and brown jasmine.

Farro: A dense, nutty grain, farro is closely related to wheat. Its texture is something between spelt and barley—and truthfully, it's similar to both. Don't use farro if you have gluten sensitivity.

Millet: My children claimed I was feeding them birdseed when I first made millet for

ARSENIC IN RICE *Years of insecticide use has left some of our most precious crops at risk for arsenic contamination. Rice is a particular concern because it very readily soaks up the arsenic in the soil. Ironically, the arsenic is prominent in the outer bran layer of rice, which is the part that is removed when brown rice is converted to white rice.*

The best choices to avoid this arsenic risk are organic sushi and basmati rice. Consumer Reports recommends up to 4.5 servings per week of these, but only 2 servings of other types of rice. To further reduce arsenic risk levels, you can rinse the raw rice thoroughly before cooking and cook the rice as you would pasta, using a ratio of 6 cups water to 1 cup rice, then drain off the remaining water afterward.
—MEHMET

them, but they eventually grew to love the tiny grain.

Oats: A nutritious breakfast staple packed with belly-filling fiber. Oats are so easy to cook they're the one thing Mehmet makes for himself.

Quinoa: Probably the grain we use most often, though technically it's a "pseudo-grain" (actually a seed). It has a great nutty flavor and light but firm consistency. Make sure you rinse off the saponin (see below) before using.

Pastas: Some of us would probably eat pasta every night if given the choice, but we try to enjoy it in moderation. When we do indulge, these are the types we prefer:

Whole wheat pasta The slightly gritty texture takes a little getting used to, but once you do, other pastas seem rather insipid.

Pastas from Italy Our family has fewer problems digesting pasta produced in Italy than that of American brands. (I have a couple of ideas as to why this may be so, mostly having to do with Europe's less pervasive use of hybrid wheat and more rigorous pesticide legislation, but I can't prove them.) For now, I go with my gut (pun intended) and stick to Italian pastas.

Japanese style noodles (udon, soba, and ramen) We use these to give texture and substance to Asian-inspired soups.

Legumes
Beans, or legumes, are a wonderful source of protein, fiber, and micronutrients. We use them frequently in everything from hearty soups to salads. They are remarkably satisfying and keep us full for hours.

Canned beans: For last-minute meals, especially soup and chili, it's handy to have a few cans in the pantry.

Dried beans: These take a little planning ahead of time—at least a few hours and sometimes overnight—but the added step of rinsing and soaking the beans actually makes them healthier. Our favorite varieties include black, red kidney, pinto, cannellini (white kidney), and chickpeas (garbanzo beans).

Lentils (red, green, or French): These are much quicker cooking than other beans and don't need to be soaked ahead of time, just rinsed.

Dry Goods
There are a few pantry products that we add to dishes to increase their nutritional value and taste.

Protein powder: We use a variety of protein powders, including whey, rice, hemp, and

SAPONIN Quinoa has a natural bitter-tasting substance called saponin on its outer skin that, when consumed, depletes the body of essential nutrients. Because the saponin dissolves when the quinoa is rinsed, many commercial brands of quinoa are prerinsed; if the product is not labeled as such, you should assume that the saponins are present. I recommend rerinsing in any case. If nothing else, you will remove any residue or other inedible material. Pour the quinoa into a fine-mesh strainer and hold the grain under cold running water while stirring it with your hands. —**MEHMET**

pea. Play around with the different types until you find one you like best.

Nutritional yeast flakes: These have a unique nutty/cheesy flavor. They are used commonly in vegan cuisine and are a good source of B vitamins.

Seaweed: A delicious source of iodine and essential minerals. When they were younger, our girls would pretend they were mermaids while eating it. They may still. We use seaweed in dishes when we want an oceanic taste without having fish. We also love it in salads or as a simple snack. Here are various types of seaweed:

Hijiki It looks like spiky twigs when dried. Though it's been shown to contain some inorganic arsenic, the level can be significantly reduced by soaking or cooking. So to make sure hijiki is properly prepared, buy it dried and rehydrate it yourself.

PHYTIC ACID Whenever we dined out in Turkey, nuts from the local trees were soaked and served on ice. I love the chewy texture and lack of bitterness, but I learned the health benefits of this only as a physician. It turns out that there are enzyme inhibitors, phytic acid and goitrogens on the surface of nuts that keep them dormant until optimal growing conditions are present. When nuts are placed in water, these harmful substances are broken down and neutralized. If nuts are eaten without soaking, the enzyme inhibitors and phytic acid can block the absorption of essential nutrients like magnesium, calcium, and zinc. This might cause intestinal irritability, mineral deficiencies, and more serious conditions over time. **—MEHMET**

Roasted nori A crispy snack alternative to chips.

Nuts and Seeds

We keep them in the pantry because we go through them quickly, but if you're not going to use nuts or seeds within two months of purchase, it's best to store them in the fridge or freezer to keep their oils from going rancid. Also, remember to soak your nuts before you eat them to maximize their nutritional value.

Almonds: Simply amazing when soaked. Honestly, it's like an entirely different nut. Once they're hydrated, keep them in the refrigerator so you can enjoy a cold, crisp, delicious snack anytime.

Cashews: These nuts are incredibly versatile, especially as a dairy substitute in vegan recipes. (Check out the cashew frosting for the carrot cake on page 229.)

Hazelnuts (filberts): These are the most popular nuts in Turkey (which produces 75 percent of the world's supply), so naturally Mehmet is a huge fan. We coarsely chop them and toss them onto salads, vegetables, and oatmeal.

Pecans: These nuts are soft and crunchy at the same time. (I know that sounds odd, but it's true.) Pecans have a warm, woodsy flavor that is wonderful with anything sweet.

Pine nuts: These have a fresh, evergreen taste, which is a nice counterpoint to their dense, fatty texture. They are especially good if you toast them in a dry skillet until lightly browned.

Walnuts: Full of healthy omega-3 essential fatty acids, these are the king of nuts—at least in our household. They have a lovely unctuous flavor with just a hint of bitter complexity.

Flaxseeds: A delicious source of omega-3 fats; when they are ground very fine and mixed with water, they make a great substitute for eggs in vegan baking.

Hemp seeds: These have a delicate, buttery flavor and soft texture; they're also a good source of protein, healthy fats, and magnesium.

Pumpkin seeds: High in zinc and vitamin E; our favorite way to eat them is tossed with a little coconut oil and salt, and roasted in the oven until crispy and golden.

Sesame seeds: We use these to add a slight crunch and a subtle, nutty flavor to Asian-inspired dishes; they supply minerals like copper and manganese.

Sunflower seeds: These are a favorite on salads and sandwiches, or just eaten by the handful as a healthy snack.

Oils

Most of the time we use only two oils but include small amounts of flavored oils to intensify the taste of some recipes.

Coconut oil: My favorite oil for cooking at higher temperatures. It's antimicrobial, has a tropical flavor, and is full of medium-chain triglycerides, which help curb your appetite and speed up your metabolism.

Extra-virgin olive oil: This is liquid gold. We literally use it every day.

Flavored oils: We use a variety of these.

Toasted sesame Gives food a wonderful, smoky, Asian taste.

Truffle-flavored Highly aromatic, this oil is like a tuxedo for food. Just a little drizzle and the food suddenly feels all dressed up.

Chili A lovely liquid heat.

Seasonings

Cardamom: You can use ground cardamom to give a somewhat flowery flavor to desserts or rice dishes. Our family likes to crush the whole pods in tea to make our Oz version of chai.

Cinnamon: Produced from the bark of a tree, cinnamon has a distinctive flavor that goes especially well with fall and winter dishes. (Think apple and pumpkin pies, spiced cider, and ginger snaps.) Cinnamon also has been shown to help control blood sugar.

Cumin: How I love this spice. It provides a warm, earthy flavor that transforms even the most mundane of dishes into something exotic.

Garlic powder: Usually we use fresh garlic, but when a subtler flavor is called for, dehydrated garlic powder is a great option.

Green chile powder: This is ground dried New Mexican chiles; it has a milder chile taste but still has a nice kick.

Nigella seeds: These tiny black seeds are also known as *kalonji;* they have a pungent, slightly bitter flavor.

Old Bay seasoning: This is a proprietary blend of spices that includes celery salt, pepper, and paprika. It's most commonly used with seafood, but it is also super-tasty sprinkled over popcorn or scrambled eggs.

Onion powder: We normally go with fresh onions, but there are instances when, in the interest of time or because I'm mixing it into dry ingredients, or when I just want a hint of onion, I reach for this powder.

Oregano: Fragrant and slightly bitter, oregano is a dominant flavor in many Italian dishes. Yep, it's that pizza taste.

Red pepper flakes: Dried bits of red chiles; it's one of our go-to spices for adding heat.

Sea salt: We stay away from regular table salt, which has preservatives and anticaking agents, including aluminum. Though we generally use a fine sea salt, we occasionally choose a coarser grain, such as Maldon or fleur de sel.

Truffle-flavored salt: It's got the opulent taste of truffles without the exorbitant price tag.

Turmeric: This vibrant yellow root has potent medicinal qualities. Cook it with ground black pepper to enhance its absorption in the body.

Wasabi powder: Also known as Japanese horseradish, wasabi is extremely pungent and has a sharp sort of heat that seems to affect your nose even more than your tongue.

Dr. Bragg's Liquid Aminos: A salty liquid seasoning made from soybeans that contains fifteen essential amino acids.

Mirin: This is a sweet rice wine commonly used in Japanese cooking.

Tamari: A wheat-free version of soy sauce made from miso paste.

Vinegars

Apple cider vinegar: Very sharp and fruity, its characteristic taste can take over a recipe if not used judiciously. We like it paired with other strong flavors like ginger.

Balsamic vinegar: Dark and sweet with a gentle acidity, this vinegar has become extremely popular for good reason.

Brown rice wine vinegar: Lightly sweet and sour, we use this in Japanese-style salad dressings.

Red wine, white wine, and champagne vinegar: These are the vinegars we use the most. We choose red when we want a perceptible tartness and the other two when we need a more understated acid note.

Sweeteners

Condensed milk: Okay, naughty food alert: nothing good for you here at all, just pure, decadent indulgence. Basically, it's milk with sugar that has been heated to evaporate its water content. At least look for organic, non-GMO brands so you won't have entirely thrown caution to the wind when you find yourself licking it off your fingers.

Evaporated cane juice: Make no mistake, this is not a health food (it is basically straight sugar), but it undergoes one less refining step than white sugar. (That last step involves surfactants, preservatives, and bleaching agents.) Even without the chemicals, this is best used in moderation.

Honey: This is our sweetener of choice for almost everything. We actually raise our own bees in the backyard. It's antimicrobial, antifungal, helps heal wounds, and helps prevents allergies (if harvested locally). Buy it from a nearby farmers' market, if possible; if not, just make sure to get it raw. Once honey is pasteurized you might as well be eating straight sugar.

Maple syrup: Make sure you use *real* maple syrup. There are a lot of maple-*flavored* syrups out there that are nothing more than corn syrup and chemicals.

Molasses (unsulfured): Thick and robust with a bold flavor, this is a by-product of sugar production and should be used sparingly.

Pomegranate molasses: Sticky, sweet, and redolent, this is a gourmet item I get online or at Middle Eastern specialty shops.

Sucanat: This proprietary product is an even less refined cane juice that still has some of the molasses in it. I prefer it to conventional brown sugar, which is just fully refined sugar coated with molasses.

Canned and Jarred Items
Check to make sure you buy canned goods that say "BPA free" on the label.

Chipotle chiles in adobo: A wonderfully smoky, hot Mexican flavor to stir into mayonnaise, chilies, soups, and casseroles.

Coconut milk: A featured ingredient in Thai cuisine; we use this in soups and curries to give them a tropical, creamy taste.

Peanut butter (organic and unsweetened): If your kids are like ours, they probably complain about the oil floating on the top of natural-style peanut butter. My trick is to stir it well when you first open it, while it is at room temperature, and after that store it in the refrigerator to keep it from separating again.

Tomato paste: Concentrated tomato flavor that you can add to recipes to create intensity. It also serves to thicken a watery sauce.

Whole and crushed tomatoes: These are a lifesaver in mid-winter, when fresh tomatoes are tasteless, mushy, and shipped thousands of miles. Canned tomatoes are also great in soups.

Dried Fruit
Apricots: They're soft and chewy with a delicate sweetness. Look for brands that don't use sulfur dioxide as a preservative.

Cherries: The perfect blend of sweet and sour, cherries are great on salads and with grains.

Dates: Delightfully sweet but also high in fiber, minerals, and vitamin K.

Shredded unsweetened coconut: We use this in desserts and as a condiment with sweet vegetables. It's high in natural sugar and fat, so we try not to overdo it.

COUNTER
Some fruits and vegetables are better when they're kept at room temperature but because of their highly perishable nature can't really be locked away in the pantry. These are the items we keep in big bowls or baskets on the kitchen counter.

Vegetables

Avocados: Smooth, creamy, and full of antioxidants and healthy fats, avocados are on the menu for breakfast, lunch, or dinner in the Oz household.

Garlic: Fiercely pungent when raw, garlic softens with a mellow sweetness when cooked.

Onions: Whether sweet, red, or yellow, onions get put raw into salads and sandwiches, and sautéed in just about everything else.

Shallots: These are like mini onions, only sweeter and more intense at the same time.

Sweet potatoes: Soft and luscious, sweet potatoes come in a variety of colors ranging from brilliant orange to pale yellow and even vivid purple.

Tomatoes: We fluctuate between keeping our tomatoes on the counter and in the fridge. Generally, if they're perfectly ripe, firm, succulent, juicy, right out of the garden, we eat them. Then, if there are any left over, they get refrigerated. Those that haven't reached their peak of perfection sit on the counter.

Winter squash (butternut, acorn, pumpkin): All rich in beta-carotene and flavor, these are prominently featured in our autumn and winter meals.

Fruits

Bananas: Smooth, sweet, and creamy, potassium-rich bananas are the number one ingredient in our breakfast smoothies.

Melons (watermelon, cantaloupe, casaba): Sweet and juicy, melons are full of nutrients but remarkably low in calories. They're best in the summer months.

Pomegranate: These gorgeous ruby-colored seeds (arils) are packed with antioxidants.

REFRIGERATOR
Dairy

Though we do eat dairy products, they are considered condiments in our home. We will sprinkle some cheese over a soup or use Greek yogurt as a vegetable dip, but we refrain from making dairy the main attraction.

Butter: Yes, it's a saturated fat, but I'll take a pat of organic butter over some chemically concocted margarine every time.

Cheese: I can try to justify my cheese habit by telling you that cheese has got protein and calcium, but the truth is, I love it because it tastes amazing. Parmigiano-Reggiano, romano, goat cheese, Haloumi, and feta (Greek/Bulgarian/French) are among our favorite cheeses. That said, we do try to keep the indulgence to a minimum.

Eggs: They're tasty, affordable, and high in protein. However, the way eggs are conventionally farmed makes us uncomfortable. Besides the obvious issues of animal cruelty, modern chicken farming involves the heavy use of antibiotics, both to fend off diseases due to overcrowding and to kill the intestinal flora of the birds, thereby stimulating rapid growth. We stick to organic, free-range, and ideally "pasture-raised" eggs, or better yet, we pick them up locally at our farmers' market.

Milk (almond milk, as vegan alternative): We use either type of milk in coffee, tea, and cereal.

Yogurt (Greek): Thick, creamy, and full of gut-healthy probiotics, this is the dairy product we use most frequently.

Meats and Proteins

Fish/poultry/meat: You won't often find these in our refrigerator, because our family eats them only a few times a week and we usually like to make a run to the market the day we're preparing them. The exceptions are frozen shrimp or chicken legs, and sliced turkey for Oliver when he craves animal protein and no one's in the mood to shop.

Miso: Made from fermented soybeans, miso has a rich, salty flavor.

Tofu (soft and firm): Though it's a good source of vegan protein, we limit our consumption of tofu to one or two meals a week because of the prevalence of phytoestrogens (which can interfere with normal hormonal function), phytates (which can prevent the absorption of some nutrients), and goitrogens (which can depress thyroid function).

Fruits

Blueberries: These vibrant berries are extraordinarily high in antioxidants and perfect for smoothies, cereals, desserts, and snacks.

Citrus: Because of their thick skins, you can generally get away with eating these non-organic. It's important, though, to buy organic citrus fruits if you're going to use the zest, because of the food coloring and pesticides found in the peel. We keep our crisper drawers full of juicy lemons, limes, grapefruits, oranges, and clementines.

Mangoes: Rich in micronutrients including enzymes, mangoes are delicious and make you feel like you've been transported to a tropical island.

Olives (Kalamata, oil-cured, Spanish): Yes, I know they don't seem like it, but technically these salty, fatty balls of luscious flavor are fruit.

Strawberries: They're high on the "Dirty Dozen" list (see page 24), so we try to find them organically grown. Strawberries are filled with vitamin C, phytonutrients, and fiber, so they are great to add to your breakfast or enjoy as a snack.

Vegetables

Asparagus: These crisp yet tender spears are loaded with the potent antioxidant glutathione.

Broccoli: Though highly nutritious, some people have problems with broccoli because of its distinctive, sulfur-like aroma. Using pungent aromatics like garlic, ginger, or onions can bring out broccoli's best side.

Brussels sprouts: These look like baby cabbages. They taste a lot like cabbage too, only with a bit more flavor.

Carrots: Crunchy and full of beta-carotene, carrots are delicious raw, but become even sweeter when lightly cooked.

Cauliflower: Like other cruciferous veggies, cauliflower is known for its numerous health benefits. Eaten raw, it is crisp and crumbly and has a slight odor, but roasted it becomes quite tender and mild.

Celery: I have to admit, celery is totally underrated in our household. We sauté it for most soups or casseroles and snack on it raw with dips like hummus or even peanut butter, but no one ever walks into the kitchen and says "Gosh, I'm really hungry for some celery." Since celery is an excellent source of vitamin K, molybdenum, and dietary fiber, maybe we should be saying that more often!

Chiles (jalapeño, cherry, serrano, etc.): We keep plenty of these "hotties" in the kitchen.

Cucumbers: We use the large, garden variety for juicing, but prefer the small, more flavorful Persian cucumbers in salads. I buy them unwaxed because that stuff is hard to get off. (Yeah, I know it's supposed to be edible, but who wants to eat wax?)

Eggplant: Soft-fleshed with a pleasantly bitter taste, eggplant is common in Middle Eastern, Italian, and Asian recipes. You'll find several recipes in the book that incorporate or feature eggplant.

Mushrooms: There are numerous edible mushrooms, each with a distinct flavor attribute and texture. Some are light and delicate while others are full-bodied and rich—almost meaty. These are a few of the more common ones we generally have in the house:

Portobello/cremini/button These are actually the same mushroom at different stages of development. The baby white version (button) is the softest and most mild tasting, the cremini is a little firmer and darker, with a more earthy taste, and the portobello is the mature stage, with a downright robust flavor.

Shiitake These have a somewhat springy consistency and a woodsy taste.

Scallions: These have a bright, oniony taste that is best enjoyed raw or lightly cooked. They are found frequently in Mexican, Vietnamese, and Chinese dishes.

Greens

Full of fiber, minerals, vitamins, and numerous health-promoting phytochemicals, dark leafy greens are among the most nutrient-dense foods on the planet. Here are some that we especially like.

Arugula: This peppery green gives depth and dimension to an otherwise bland salad.

Kale: What can I possibly say about kale? It's a superfood! It's the most talked about vegetable of the last decade—and deservedly so.

Romaine: Packed with nutrients like vitamins K and A, these long, crisp leaves stand up to even the most assertive salad dressings.

Spinach: Like the other greens listed here, spinach is extremely low in calories and high in nutrient value. We try to eat it as often as possible by using it in juices and smoothies, soups, salads, or just steamed with a little olive oil and garlic.

Fresh Herbs

Basil: Fresh basil is one of the best herbs ever. Dried basil? The worst (at least according to every member of our family).

Chives: Pungent, yet clean and slightly grassy, chives provide all the fun of an onion without the hangover.

Cilantro: I would put this on just about everything, except half the family thinks it tastes like soap. It's an effective natural chelator, pulling heavy metals from the body.

Dill: Beautiful and frilly with a slight licorice flavor; we use dill most frequently with seafood or in salads.

Ginger (fresh): This succulent root provides a sharp, bright, zesty flavor.

Mint: When I was growing up, mint was reserved for iced tea, but now I toss it into salads, put it on sandwiches, and use it on pasta. If you're adding it to cooked dishes, do so at the very end.

Oregano: A wonderful savory herb that has medicinal benefits including antimicrobial properties.

Parsley: It has a fresh flavor that adds interest to rice, pastas, and soups and is a powerful diuretic that helps flush excess water from the body.

Rosemary: This herb tastes a little like a pine tree—in a really good way. The leaves tend to be a bit spiky, so I prefer to chop them well before adding to dishes.

Thyme: I use a lot of thyme— maybe too much. But I love its aromatic, woodsy flavor. I prefer to use only the leaves, so I remove them by running two fingers backwards up the stem.

Condiments

Dijon mustard: Typically spicy but not overly hot, we frequently use this in salad dressings to bind the oil and vinegar, producing a rich, creamy texture.

Horseradish: Pungent and slightly bitter, horseradish can be grated easily and stored in vinegar and salt, or just buy it already prepared. It is thought to have great medicinal value and is used to treat sinusitis, bronchitis, and urinary tract infections.

Red and green curry pastes: These are thick Thai curries that are best in dishes made with coconut milk. You can vary the amount to control the heat in a recipe.

Sriracha: A Thai red chili sauce with a nice balance of heat. If you are vegan, check the ingredient label as some brands add shrimp paste.

Tahini: Made from ground sesame seeds, this thick paste is a staple in Middle Eastern cuisine.

Vegenaise: This brand of vegan mayonnaise tastes great and is GMO free. Its mild flavor makes it the perfect base for mixing in flavors like chipotle or wasabi to dress up your favorite sandwich.

FREEZER

These are some of the freezer items we like to have on hand:

Edamame: These are ideal for last-minute meals or snacks when you haven't had time to go food shopping. You can buy edamame shelled or in the pod, but either way I recommend buying organic.

Ezekiel bread: Ninety percent of the time this is the only bread we have in the house. It's made from a combination of sprouted grains and legumes, has no preservatives, and is completely organic. We store it in the freezer.

Frozen berries and bananas: These are the best for making smoothies. Make sure to wash and dry the berries, and peel and cut the banana before freezing.

Flours

Since we use flour only occasionally, we keep it in the freezer instead of the pantry.

Almond flour: This is a delicious gluten-free option for baking, but we use it in moderation because it is incredibly dense and contains enzyme inhibitors. Used as an occasional treat, it's great.

Coconut flour: A gluten-free flour for baking, it's made from dried coconut meat and has a naturally sweet flavor.

Gluten-free baking mix: While there are several brands out there, our favorite is Bob's Red Mill. It's a blend of garbanzo bean flour, potato starch, whole-grain white sorghum flour, tapioca flour, and fava bean flour.

White all-purpose flour (unbleached): We use this very, very rarely. Generally it's for birthday cakes, holiday pies, and a special-occasion batch of chocolate chip cookies.

Whole wheat flour: We use whole wheat flour for most of our baking needs, from homemade crackers to pancakes and muffins.

THE TOOLS

I want to touch on equipment. This is such a personal thing. People have specific brands of knives they prefer or certain types of pots. I happen to be particularly attached to well-worn, long, thin-handled wooden spoons. I like the way the smooth shaft fits in my hand and the fact that I can stir a soup without getting too close to the heat. I only mention this because once, when Mehmet's team was shooting a segment in our kitchen, they threw out all my old, shabby, food-stained spoons and replaced them with brand-new ones. Sadly, the new ones were short and stumpy with thick, scratchy wood handles. I was furious—and over such a trivial thing. But people become very attached to their cooking tools. With that in mind (and without overhauling your kitchen), these are a few things we utilize in the Oz household to make preparing meals a little more healthful, efficient, and manageable.

A good water filter: We use filtered water for all our cooking. Don't get me wrong; modern water treatment in the United States is a miraculous thing. It's had a tremendous impact on public health over the last 100 years by drastically reducing pathogens like giardia and cryptosporidium—scary-sounding things you do not want in your water. I'm extremely grateful to live in a country that provides its citizens with access to safe water. That being said, there are still many contaminants that are unregulated by the Environmental Protection Agency and therefore remain in our drinking water. Additionally, by-products of the chlorination treatment or added chemicals (like fluoride) are potentially toxic. A good water filter can help reduce those toxins. Home options range from very affordable carbon filters (simply a pitcher you keep in your fridge) to quite expensive whole-house, reverse-osmosis systems.

A juicer: Fresh juice is a great way to increase nutrient intake, and besides, we love the way it tastes. For me, the real problem with juicing is the cleanup. If that's a bother for you, too, find a model that has machine-washable parts. Another thing to look for is a wide feed tube so you don't need to spend a lot of time cutting your fruits and vegetables into small pieces. Also, if you're going to be juicing a ton of leafy greens or wheat grass, go for a cold-press (auger-style) juicer, which works by pressing and crushing the produce.

A heavy-duty blender: A good blender is essential for everything from smoothies to soups. I even use it to make my favorite vegan icing. But don't feel that you need to run out and spend a ton of money on a top-of-the-line brand. Blenders are wonderful machines, but there are a lot of less expensive ones that work just as well for meeting a home cook's needs. Honestly, don't get caught up in having to have the fanciest gadgets; I use my Ninja more than anything else.

Nontoxic cookware: Nonstick pans seem like a home cook's best friend because they eliminate so much of the mess of dishwashing, but they really aren't a great choice. Teflon pans emit toxic fumes at high temperatures, and the aluminum in some pans can leach into food as it cooks. While cast-iron, ceramic-lined, and stainless steel are the healthiest options, there are nights when I just don't feel like scrubbing after dinner so we have "green" pans that are made without PFOA (perfluorooctanoic acid) or PTFE (polytetrafluoroethylene). If you're going to go with aluminum, make sure it's anodized aluminum.

Sharp knives: By no means is it a requirement, but I urge you to keep your knives sharp. I used dull knives for years, until a kid from Daphne's school came by selling knife sets door to door. She gave a presentation worthy of an infomercial and I was blown away by the difference a good cutting instrument could make. I ended up with a drawer full, in every length and style. They've lasted now for over a decade, and every time I feel they are losing their edge, I run them over to a nearby hardware store where they get a quick, inexpensive tune-up.

That pretty much sums up what we've got in our kitchen. Please use these lists as inspiration, but don't be limited by them. These are the things *we* like, but what you use is up to you. As you shop for your foods, try to make choices that are natural, whole, and abundant with life's energy. Find items that excite you, that make you want to cook and eat and celebrate. Feed your family. Nourish your soul. Fill *your* kitchen with the things you love.

BREAKFAST

I grew up just outside of Philadelphia, birthplace of the famous (or infamous) Philly cheesesteak. Though I gave up beef decades ago, I still have a fondness for the sizzling sub—mostly because Mehmet took me to a cheesesteak joint on our very first date. The combination of sautéed vegetables and melted Muenster on a baguette turns a simple egg sandwich into a taste of home.

PHILLY FRIED EGGS with ONIONS and PEPPERS

MAKES 6 SERVINGS

4 tablespoons extra-virgin olive oil

1 large sweet onion, cut into rings

2 medium red bell peppers, cut into rings, seeds and ribs removed

1 teaspoon dried oregano

Fine sea salt and freshly ground black pepper

1 baguette

6 slices Muenster cheese

6 large eggs

Heat 1 tablespoon of the oil in a large skillet over medium-high heat. Add the onion, bell peppers, and oregano. Season to taste with salt and pepper. Cook until the vegetables are very tender, 12 to 15 minutes. Transfer to a medium bowl and cover with aluminum foil.

Position the broiler rack about 6 inches from the source of heat and preheat the broiler.

Cut the baguette almost in half lengthwise and open it up like a book. Cut the baguette crosswise into six equal pieces. Broil the bread pieces, cut sides open, until toasted, about 1 minute. Cover each piece of bread with the cheese and broil until melted, about 30 seconds more. Remove from the broiler. Place each cheese-topped toast on a dinner plate. Divide the bell pepper mixture evenly over the toasts.

Divide the remaining 3 tablespoons oil between two large skillets, preferably nonstick, and heat over medium-high heat. Crack the eggs into the skillets and cover. Cook until the egg whites are set, about 2 minutes for sunny-side up. If desired, turn the eggs over and cook for about 30 seconds more for over-easy eggs. Season the eggs with salt and pepper. Top each toast with a fried egg and serve.

When we visit Mehmet's parents in Turkey, breakfast is a sumptuous celebration of flavors, both savory and sweet. It's a buffet-style combination of fruit, cheese, eggs, and vegetables, served with a crusty slice of warm toast. We linger for hours around this feast while overlooking the historic waterway dividing Europe from Asia. For us, this is the perfect melding of East and West.

BOSPHORUS BREAKFAST with SOFT-BOILED EGGS and FRUIT

MAKES 6 SERVINGS

6 large eggs

3 Persian or Israeli cucumbers, cut lengthwise into quarters

2 large ripe tomatoes, cut into wedges

1 pound feta cheese in a block, drained, cut into ½-inch slices

1 cup oil-cured black olives, such as Gaeta

Extra-virgin olive oil, as needed

Fine sea salt

6 slices pale-fleshed melon, such as honeydew or crenshaw

2 ripe peaches, cut into wedges

8 ounces fresh Bing cherries

Raw honey, as needed

6 slices sprouted wheat bread

Place the eggs in a bowl and cover with hot tap water. Let the eggs stand to lose their chill while assembling the rest of the breakfast, about 10 minutes. Meanwhile, add enough cold water to come 2 inches up the side of a large, wide saucepan. Cover and bring the water to a boil over high heat.

Position a rack in the center of the oven and preheat the oven to 200°F.

(recipe continues)

EGGS *The whites of eggs are a great source of protein, but the yolks are where most of the nutrients are stored, including vitamins A, B, D, and E. The yolk is also rich in choline, which helps promote brain and liver function, and lutein and zeaxanthin, which help keep the eyes healthy.* **—MEHMET**

Arrange the cucumbers, tomatoes, feta, and olives in small bowls or on a platter. Drizzle them with oil and season with salt. Arrange the melon, peaches, and cherries in bowls or on another platter and drizzle them with honey.

To soft-boil the eggs, using a large slotted spoon, one at a time, carefully place the eggs in the water, and return to the boil. Reduce the heat to medium-low. Cook the eggs at a steady simmer for 4 minutes. Using the spoon, transfer each egg to an eggcup (or some other vessel to hold it upright, such as a shot glass).

Meanwhile, toast the bread in the oven, directly on the oven rack.

Serve everything in the center of the table and invite each person to fill his or her plate with individual selections.

In this dish, the earthiness of the mushrooms is enhanced by creamy goat cheese and aromatic thyme. You can use just about any mushroom combination you like—cremini, button, oyster, chanterelles, and so on. Adjust the cooking time as needed because some mushrooms give up more liquid than others.

MUSHROOM and GOAT CHEESE FRITTATA

MAKES 6 SERVINGS

2 tablespoons extra-virgin olive oil

10 ounces button mushrooms, sliced

4 ounces fresh shiitake mushrooms, stems discarded and caps sliced, or additional button mushrooms

Fine sea salt and freshly ground black pepper

1/4 cup finely chopped shallots

1 teaspoon finely chopped fresh thyme, plus thyme sprigs for garnish

1/2 teaspoon dried oregano

9 large eggs

3/4 cup crumbled rindless goat cheese (3 ounces)

Position the broiler rack about 8 inches from the source of heat and preheat the broiler.

Heat the oil in a large nonstick skillet with a heatproof handle (or wrap the handle in aluminum foil) over medium-high heat. Add the button and shiitake mushrooms and season with 1/4 teaspoon salt and a few grinds of pepper. Cook, stirring occasionally, until the mushroom liquid has evaporated, about 8 minutes. Stir in the shallots, thyme, and oregano and cook, stirring occasionally, until the shallots are tender, about 2 minutes more.

Whisk the eggs with 1/2 teaspoon salt and 1/4 teaspoon pepper in a large bowl until combined. Pour into the skillet over the mushrooms. Reduce the heat to medium. Cook until the egg mixture is set around the edges, about 1 minute. Using a heatproof spatula, lift up the set edges of the frittata and tilt the pan to let the uncooked egg mixture flow underneath the cooked portion. Continue cooking, occasionally tilting the pan as before, until the frittata is set but shiny on top, 2 to 3 minutes more.

Transfer the skillet with the frittata to the broiler and broil just until the frittata is puffed and golden, about

1 minute. Remove from the broiler and immediately sprinkle the goat cheese over the frittata. Turn off the broiler. Return the frittata to the broiler to lightly melt the goat cheese, about 1 minute. Remove from the broiler again and let cool slightly. Cut into wedges, garnish with the thyme sprigs, and serve.

GOAT CHEESE is rich in thiamine, riboflavin, niacin, and vitamin K. It is a staple in Turkey, where I spent a quarter of my childhood. Compared to most types of cheese made from cow's milk, goat cheese has fewer calories per ounce and approximately half the salt, fat, and cholesterol. It's also easier to digest because the fat proteins are smaller, resembling those of human milk. So if you're sensitive to cow's milk dairy, you may want to give goat cheese a try.
—MEHMET

GARLIC lowers blood pressure and improves blood cholesterol levels. (*Eating half a clove of garlic a day can reduce cholesterol by nearly 10 percent.*) *It helps detoxify the body and boost the immune system, and garlic has been shown to reduce the severity of illnesses like the common cold and the flu.* —**MEHMET**

This is Arabella's favorite breakfast. It's quick but somehow feels special. That little drizzle of truffle oil makes anything seem sumptuous, almost decadent. This is a fabulous dish to serve for a romantic breakfast in bed.

POACHED EGGS ON GARLIC TOAST with TRUFFLE OIL and JALAPEÑO

MAKES 6 SERVINGS

2 tablespoons cider vinegar

6 large eggs

6 slices sprouted wheat bread

1 or 2 large garlic cloves, cut in half crosswise

6 teaspoons white truffle-flavored oil, as needed

Fine sea salt

2 jalapeños, seeded and minced

Position a rack in the center of the oven and preheat the oven to 200°F.

Bring 3 quarts of lightly salted water and the vinegar to a boil in a large saucepan over high heat. Fill a large bowl with hot tap water and place it near the stove. Reduce the heat to medium-low to keep the water at a simmer.

For each egg, crack the egg into the simmering water. Using a large slotted spoon, move the egg white over the rest of the egg to give it a neater shape as it sets. Simmer until the egg white is opaque but the yolk is liquid, about 1½ minutes. With a little practice, you can cook two or three eggs at a time—just keep track of the timing for each egg. Using the spoon, carefully lift out the egg and transfer it to the bowl of hot water to keep warm.

Toast the bread in the oven. For each serving, rub the cut side of the garlic all over one side of each toast.

Place the toast, garlic side up, on a plate. Using the slotted spoon, gently remove an egg from the water and drain it briefly. Transfer to the toast. Drizzle about a teaspoon of the truffle oil over the egg and toast. Sprinkle with the salt and jalapeño. Serve immediately.

We make this dish on Sunday mornings when the whole family is home for the weekend. It's quick and easily expandable, should unexpected friends drop by (which is always a possibility when you've got teenagers). It's also super-satisfying, so we don't need to worry about lunch for hours.

EGGS with MEXICAN BLACK BEANS

MAKES 4 SERVINGS

BLACK BEANS

1 tablespoon extra-virgin olive oil

½ cup finely chopped shallots

1 jalapeño, seeded and minced

1 teaspoon dried thyme

1 teaspoon dried oregano

Two 15-ounce cans black beans, drained and rinsed

Fine sea salt and freshly ground black pepper

EGGS

8 large eggs

3 tablespoons finely chopped fresh chives

1 teaspoon garlic powder

½ teaspoon fine sea salt

2 teaspoons extra-virgin olive oil

2 ripe Hass avocados, sliced

Chopped fresh cilantro, for serving

Hot pepper sauce, preferably Mexican, for serving

To make the beans: Heat the oil in a medium saucepan over medium heat. Add the shallots and jalapeño. Cook, stirring occasionally, until the shallots are tender but not browned, about 2 minutes. Stir in the thyme and oregano. Add the beans and ⅓ cup water. Cook, stirring occasionally, until the beans are heated through and most of the liquid has evaporated, about 5 minutes. Season to taste with salt and pepper. Remove from the heat and cover to keep warm.

To make the eggs: Whisk the eggs, chives, garlic powder, and salt together in a large bowl just until combined. Heat the oil in a large skillet over medium heat. Add the egg mixture and cook, stirring occasionally with a wooden spoon, just until the eggs are scrambled and set, 2 to 3 minutes.

For each serving, spoon the beans and eggs next to each other on a plate. Add the sliced avocado and a sprinkle of cilantro. Serve with the hot sauce passed on the side.

When Mehmet and I visited India, we were enthralled with the exotic flavors and colors of the local cuisine. The turmeric and cumin in this scramble are reminiscent of our favorite dishes from that trip.

INDIAN TOFU and VEGETABLE SCRAMBLE

MAKES 4 SERVINGS

2 tablespoons coconut oil

½ large sweet onion, chopped

1 medium red bell pepper, cored and cut into ½-inch dice

1 jalapeño, seeded and finely chopped

2 garlic cloves, minced

2 tablespoons finely chopped fresh oregano

1 teaspoon ground turmeric

1 teaspoon ground cumin

One 14-ounce package extra-firm tofu, drained and pressed (see Note)

Fine sea salt and freshly ground black pepper

Heat the oil in a large skillet over medium-high heat. Add the onion, bell pepper, and jalapeño. Cook, stirring occasionally, until the vegetables are tender and beginning to brown, about 5 minutes. Stir in the garlic and cook, stirring often, until fragrant, about 1 minute. Stir in the oregano, turmeric, and cumin.

Crumble the tofu into the skillet. Cook, stirring occasionally, until the tofu is heated through, about 3 minutes. Season to taste with salt and pepper. Serve hot.

NOTE To get the best results when cooking tofu, you need to remove the excess water. To do this, line a dinner plate with a double thickness of paper towels and place the tofu block on the plate. Top the tofu with more paper towels and a second plate. Weight the top plate down with a few heavy cans of food. Let the setup stand 15 to 20 minutes. While the tofu is being pressed, you can prepare the vegetables for the recipe. However, when I am in a hurry, I rush things with a hands-on method: Hold the tofu block between your hands and firmly squeeze it to press out the liquid without crushing the tofu. Pat the block very dry with paper towels before cooking.

TURMERIC is a commonly used medicinal tool in the ancient Indian healing tradition of Ayurveda. Rich in curcumin, it has been shown to have antioxidant, antiseptic, and anti-inflammatory properties. Studies also suggest curcumin may protect against cancer and Alzheimer's disease. —**MEHMET**

This breakfast recipe is actually based on a dessert—sticky rice with mango. Zoe spent a summer working at a hospital in Thailand and practically lived on the stuff. When she came home, we made this healthier version for breakfast and she was hooked. She prefers rolled oats, but you could easily substitute the steel-cut variety.

THAI OATMEAL with MANGO and COCONUT MILK

MAKES 1 SERVING

Pinch of fine sea salt

½ cup old-fashioned rolled oats

½ mango, peeled, seeded, and cut into bite-size cubes

⅓ cup canned coconut milk (not cream of coconut)

Pure maple syrup, for serving

Bring 1 cup water and the salt to a boil in a small saucepan over high heat. Stir in the oats and reduce the heat to medium-low. Simmer, stirring occasionally, until the oats are almost tender, 4 to 5 minutes. Remove from the heat, cover tightly, and let stand for 2 minutes.

Spoon the oatmeal into a cereal bowl. Top with the mango and coconut milk. Serve immediately, with the maple syrup to taste.

MANGOES are great for your digestion. They are high in fiber to aid in elimination and contain enzymes that help break down protein. They also provide all of your minimum daily vitamin C needs and help prevent periodontal disease. —**MEHMET**

When Oliver was in middle school, he had to do a report on gladiators that included what they ate before entering the arena. We thought it might be fun to try to replicate that mix of grains and dried fruit seasoned with fresh herbs and salted meat. (We used a soy-based Canadian bacon.) Now it's his breakfast of choice to fuel up before Saturday football games.

"GLADIATOR" IRISH OATMEAL
with SOY BACON, DATES, and ROSEMARY

MAKES 4 SERVINGS

1 cup steel-cut (Irish) oats

Pinch of fine sea salt

1 tablespoon coconut oil

4 ounces soy Canadian bacon slices, cut into bite-size pieces

10 to 12 dates, pitted and coarsely chopped

3 tablespoons finely chopped shallots

2 teaspoons finely chopped fresh rosemary

Red pepper flakes or freshly ground black pepper

Bring 4 cups water, the oats, and salt to a boil in a medium, heavy-bottomed saucepan over high heat. Reduce the heat to low and simmer, taking care to stir them just to prevent sticking to the bottom of the saucepan, until the oats are tender, about 20 minutes.

Meanwhile, melt the oil in a medium skillet over medium-high heat. Add the soy bacon and cook, stirring occasionally, until the bacon is beginning to crisp, about 3 minutes. Add the dates, shallots, and rosemary and reduce the heat to medium. Cook, stirring often, until the shallots are tender, about 2 minutes. Season the mixture with the red pepper flakes. Remove from the heat.

Stir all the sautéed ingredients into the cooked oatmeal, spoon into four individual bowls, and serve.

OATMEAL has so much insoluble fiber that you will be full all morning. Plus, we have appreciated for fifty years that this food specifically helps reduce cholesterol. As a bonus, you get lots of minerals without too many calories. I personally love the texture of oatmeal when it's not overcooked. —MEHMET

We love this grain-free version of granola—especially
served as a parfait layered with plain Greek yogurt and a
generous sprinkle of fresh pomegranate seeds. Add raisins,
dried cherries, or dried cranberries for some sweetness.

NO-GRAIN NUTTY GRANOLA

**MAKES ABOUT
5 CUPS**

3 tablespoons coconut oil

3 tablespoons honey

3 tablespoons pure
maple syrup

1 teaspoon vanilla extract

1 teaspoon ground
cinnamon

1 cup natural almonds,
very coarsely chopped
(4 ounces)

1 cup walnuts, very
coarsely chopped
(4 ounces)

1/2 cup raw cashews, very
coarsely chopped
(2 ounces)

1/2 cup unsweetened
shredded coconut
(1½ ounces)

1/2 cup hulled pumpkin
seeds (about 2 ounces)

1/4 cup hulled sunflower
seeds (about 1 ounce)

2 tablespoons sesame
seeds

2 tablespoons flaxseeds

Position a rack in the center of the oven and preheat the
oven to 400°F. Line a large rimmed baking sheet with
parchment paper or a silicone baking mat.

Heat the coconut oil, honey, and maple syrup together in
a large saucepan over medium heat, whisking often, until
the oil is melted and the mixture is combined. Remove
from the heat and whisk in the vanilla and cinnamon.
Add the almonds, walnuts, cashews, coconut, pumpkin
seeds, sunflower seeds, sesame seeds, and flaxseeds and
stir well to coat. Spread the mixture on the baking sheet.

Bake, stirring two or three times during cooking to
incorporate the outer edges (which cook more quickly)
with the rest of the granola, until the granola is golden
brown, 15 to 20 minutes. Remove from the oven and let
cool. Using your hands, break up the granola into small,
bite-size pieces. (Store at room temperature for up to
2 weeks.)

*COCONUT OIL contains lauric acid, which has been shown
to kill pathogens like bacteria, viruses, and yeast and to
help improve cholesterol levels. Though it is a saturated
fat, coconut oil consists of medium-chain fatty acids that
are more easily metabolized in the liver.* —MEHMET

For the most part, we prefer savory breakfasts to sweet ones. However, these protein-packed muffins are the exception to the rule. They take a little more time, but you can also freeze the leftovers and reheat them for busy school days—of course, that's if there *are* any leftovers.

BANANA, DATE, and NUT MUFFINS

MAKES 16 MUFFINS

1 cup mashed ripe bananas
(about 3 bananas)

One 7-ounce container
plain Greek yogurt
(3/4 cup plus 2 tablespoons)

1 large egg

2 tablespoons coconut
oil, melted

1 teaspoon vanilla extract

1 cup whole wheat flour

1 cup old-fashioned
rolled oats

2/3 cup packed light
brown sugar

1/2 cup unbleached
all-purpose flour

1/4 cup unflavored protein
powder

2 teaspoons baking soda

1/4 teaspoon fine sea salt

3/4 cup chopped walnuts
(3 ounces)

3/4 cup pitted and
chopped dates

Position a rack in the center of the oven and preheat the oven to 375°F. Line 16 muffin cups with paper liners.

Whisk the mashed bananas, yogurt, egg, coconut oil, and vanilla together in a medium bowl. Whisk the whole wheat flour, oats, brown sugar, all-purpose flour, protein powder, baking soda, and salt together in a large bowl, being sure to break up any clumps of brown sugar and baking soda. Add the banana mixture and stir with a wooden spoon (do not whisk) just until the batter is moistened but still lumpy. Add the walnuts and dates and mix just until the batter is combined.

Divide the batter evenly among the muffin cups. Bake until the muffins are golden brown and the tops spring back when pressed with a fingertip, 18 to 22 minutes. Let the muffins cool in the pan for 10 minutes. Remove from the pan and serve warm or cooled to room temperature.

BANANAS help with blood pressure by counterbalancing all the salt in our diets with their abundant potassium. They can also help with depression because of their high levels of tryptophan, which is rapidly converted into serotonin, the "happiness" brain neurotransmitter. —**MEHMET**

When the girls were in high school this was the go-to breakfast pretty much every morning. It's packed with protein, fiber, and the brain-boosting benefits of omega-3-rich flaxseed oil. We freeze the fruit so we don't need to add ice. (Just make sure to peel and cut up the bananas beforehand, as it's hard to get the peels off once they're frozen.)

BANANA-BLUEBERRY BREAKFAST SMOOTHIE

MAKES 1 SERVING

1 cup ice water

1/2 ripe banana, cut into chunks, preferably frozen

1/3 cup unflavored whey protein powder

1/4 cup frozen blueberries

1/2 tablespoon honey

1/2 tablespoon flaxseed oil

1 teaspoon psyllium seed husks

Process the ice water, banana, protein powder, blueberries, honey, flaxseed oil, and psyllium husks in a blender until smooth. Pour into a glass and serve immediately.

FROZEN FRUITS AND VEGETABLES have been harvested close to their peak of ripeness, when they are most nutrient dense, and flash-frozen to preserve around 85 percent of that nutrient value. Fresh produce is often picked before it is ripe, and loses some vitamin content during shipping and while on the shelf in the grocery store. Ideally, you buy local produce in season, but frozen is a convenient, economical, and nutritious alternative. —MEHMET

SOUPS AND SANDWICHES

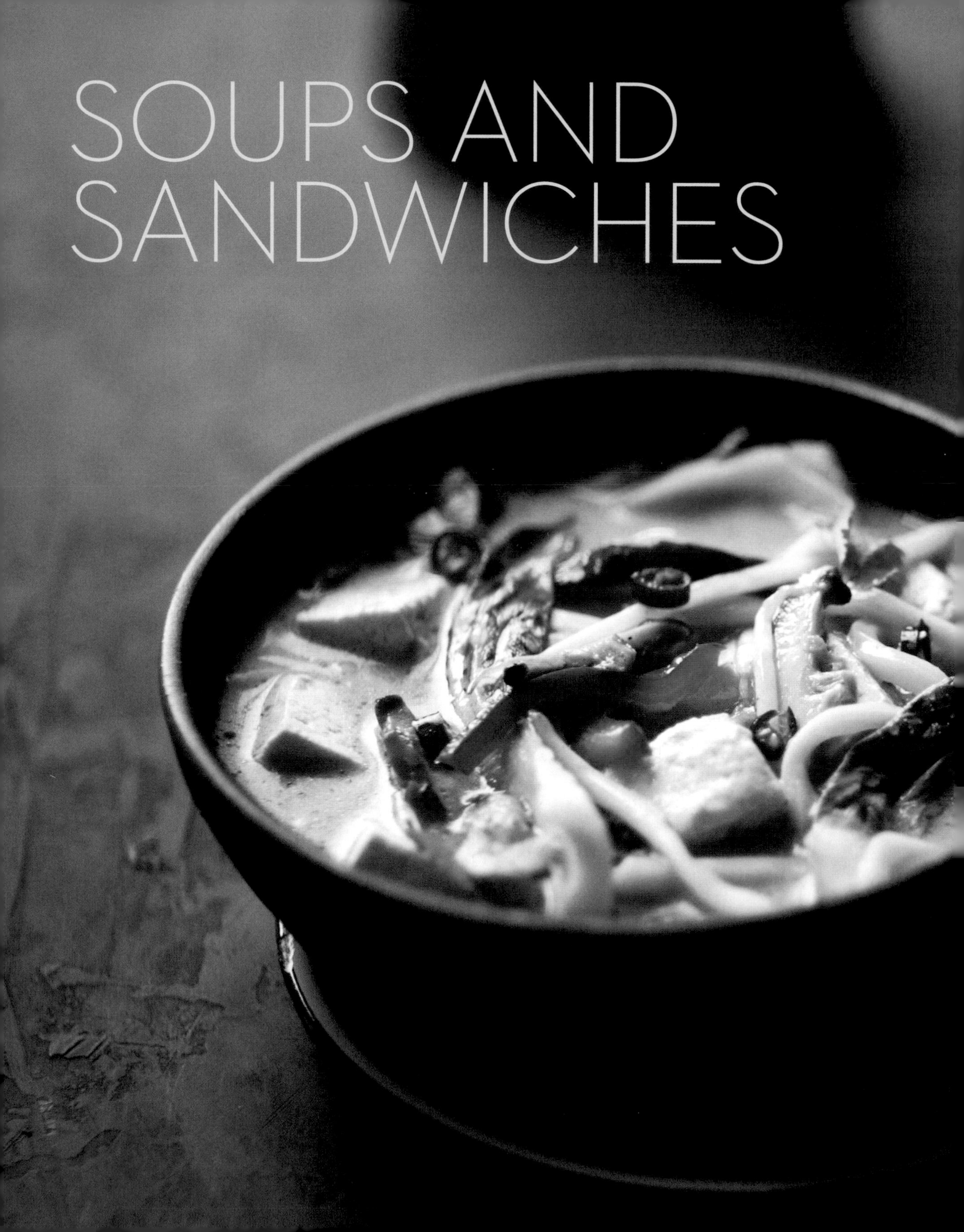

I call this "wagababy" because it is the descendant of a luscious noodle soup we first had at London's famed Wagamama restaurant. Its spicy coconut milk and sautéed veggies are a brilliant base for "add-ins." My choice is always tofu, but feel free to opt for shrimp or chicken.

"WAGABABY" POT with UDON and ASIAN VEGETABLES

MAKES 4 TO 6 SERVINGS

BROTH

2 scallions

2 tablespoons coconut oil

½ large sweet onion, chopped

1 lemongrass stalk, thick outer layer and tops removed, tender inner bulb minced

1 small hot fresh chile, such as Thai or serrano, seeded and minced

2 tablespoons vegetarian green curry paste

One 14-ounce can coconut milk

2 tablespoons tamari

NOODLES

8 to 10 ounces dried udon (see Note)

TOFU

2 teaspoons coconut oil

7 ounces extra-firm tofu, pressed (see Note, page 50), cut into ¾-inch cubes, or other "add-in" protein of choice

VEGETABLES

1 tablespoon coconut oil

1 small red bell pepper, cored and cut into ½-inch dice

6 ounces fresh shiitake mushrooms, stemmed, caps thinly sliced

2 Shanghai (baby) bok choy (about 7 ounces total)

Sea salt and freshly ground black pepper

SERVING

2 cups fresh bean sprouts (about 6 ounces total)

1 small hot red chile, such as Thai or serrano, cut into thin rounds

2 scallions (reserved dark green tops only), thinly sliced

2 tablespoons finely chopped fresh cilantro

Tamari

Chili oil

Lime wedges

BOK CHOY This Chinese cabbage contains a large number of antioxidant vitamins, like K, C, and A, to help keep the immune system strong. It also provides minerals like selenium, phosphorous, magnesium, and zinc. —MEHMET

NOTE Udon comes in packages that range from 8.8 to 9.5 ounces. If you like a lot of noodles, you can even use the larger 12-ounce package. The noodles are often tied into individual bundles that equal the standard Japanese single serving, but you can ignore the portioning for this recipe.

To make the broth: Finely chop the scallions; reserve the dark green tops for garnish. Melt the oil in a large saucepan over medium heat. Add the onion, chopped scallion, lemongrass, and chile and cook uncovered, stirring occasionally, until the onion softens, about 3 minutes. Add the curry paste and stir well.

Stir in 4 cups of water, the coconut milk, and the tamari. Bring the soup to a boil over high heat. Reduce the heat to low and simmer, about 45 minutes.

To cook the noodles: Meanwhile, bring a large pot of water to a boil over high heat. Add the udon and cook according to the package directions. Drain and rinse under cold running water. Transfer the udon to a large bowl, cover with cold water, and set aside.

To brown the tofu: Melt the oil in a medium skillet over medium-high heat Add the tofu cubes and cook, turning them occasionally, until they are golden brown, about 5 minutes. Transfer the tofu to paper towels and set aside.

To make the vegetables: Melt the oil in a large skillet over medium-high heat. Add the bell pepper and mushrooms and cook until the pepper begins to soften, about 1 minute. Add the bok choy and cook about 3 minutes more. Season to taste with the salt and pepper.

Strain the broth through a fine-mesh sieve over a large bowl, discarding the solids in the sieve. Return the broth to the saucepan and stir in the vegetables. Bring the soup to a simmer over high heat. Remove from the heat.

Thinly slice the reserved scallion tops. Drain the udon. Ladle the soup into bowls and divide the udon and tofu among them. Sprinkle each serving with bean sprouts, chile rounds, scallion tops, and cilantro. Serve, with the tamari, chili oil, and lime wedges on the side.

This light and flavorful broth is a lifesaver when I'm trying to stick to a liquid cleanse. Though I love fruit and vegetable juices, after the first day of fasting I find myself craving something savory. The miso and tamari give this a slight saltiness that helps keep my electrolytes balanced and my taste buds happy.

MISO and VEGETABLE FASTING BROTH

MAKES ABOUT 3 QUARTS

1/2 large sweet onion, coarsely chopped

1 small russet potato, peeled and cut into 2-inch chunks

3 medium carrots, coarsely chopped

2 small celery ribs, coarsely chopped

1 ounce dried mushrooms, such as porcini, or an assortment (about 1 cup loosely packed)

One 1-inch piece fresh ginger, coarsely chopped

12 garlic cloves, crushed and peeled

2 tablespoons loosely packed fresh cilantro leaves and stems

1 lemongrass stalk, thick outer layer and tops removed, tender inner bulb coarsely chopped

3/4 cup canned coconut milk

1/3 cup white (shiro) miso

2 tablespoons liquid aminos, such as Bragg's

2 tablespoons tamari

1/2 teaspoon cayenne pepper

1/2 teaspoon ground cumin

1/2 teaspoon ground coriander

Combine all of the ingredients in a very large stockpot and add 5 quarts water. Bring the mixture to a boil over high heat.

Reduce the heat to medium-low. Cook, stirring occasionally, until the broth has reduced to approximately 4 quarts, about 2½ hours. Strain the broth through a fine-mesh sieve into a large bowl. Let cool until tepid.

Transfer to covered containers. Refrigerate for up to 3 days or freeze for up to 3 months. Reheat before serving.

MISO has been a staple in Asian diets for 2,500 years; it is believed that miso stimulates digestive fluids in the stomach. It also contains all of the essential amino acids, which makes it a complete protein. As a bonus, eating miso helps you reduce the risk for several cancers and strengthens your immune system. —MEHMET

This is a remarkably satisfying soup. It's not thick, but the beans make it feel substantial and the spinach adds nice vibrancy. For a vegan meal, omit the Parmigiano cheese.

WHITE BEAN and SPINACH SOUP

MAKES 6 TO 8 SERVINGS

2 tablespoons extra-virgin olive oil

1 medium yellow onion, chopped

1 large carrot, cut into ½-inch dice

1 large celery rib, cut into ½-inch dice

2 garlic cloves, minced

1 teaspoon finely chopped fresh rosemary

1 teaspoon finely chopped fresh thyme

2 dried bay leaves

Two 15-ounce cans cannellini (white kidney beans), drained, but not rinsed

2 bunches fresh leaf spinach (about 14 ounces total), tough stems discarded, leaves well rinsed and cut into shreds

2 teaspoons fresh lemon juice

1 teaspoon pure maple syrup

¼ teaspoon red pepper flakes

Fine sea salt and freshly ground black pepper

Freshly grated Parmigiano-Reggiano cheese, for serving

Heat the oil in a large saucepan over medium heat. Add the onion, carrot, celery, and garlic and cook, stirring occasionally, until the onion is tender but not browned, about 4 minutes. Stir in the rosemary, thyme, and bay leaves. Add enough water (about 6 cups) to cover the ingredients and bring it to a boil over high heat. Reduce the heat to medium-low and cover the saucepan with the lid ajar. Simmer until the vegetables are very tender, about 30 minutes.

Stir in the beans, spinach, lemon juice, maple syrup, and red pepper flakes. Add more water, if needed, to cover the ingredients. Season the soup to taste with salt and pepper. Increase the heat to high to return the soup to a simmer. Reduce the heat to medium-low and simmer, uncovered, until the spinach is very tender and the soup is lightly thickened, about 10 minutes. Remove the bay leaves.

Ladle the soup into bowls and serve hot, with the Parmigiano passed on the side for sprinkling.

SPINACH is packed with essential minerals and vitamins and powerful antioxidants. It can lower blood pressure, improve bone health, and help control blood glucose levels in diabetics. —MEHMET

BUTTERNUT SQUASH is a great source of beta-carotene, which contains powerful antioxidant and anti-inflammatory properties. One cup of squash provides over 50 percent of your daily vitamin C needs, more potassium than a banana, and a healthy dose of fiber. —MEHMET

One of the things we love about fall is the abundance of butternut squash. This recipe, with a dash of ginger and a soupçon of maple syrup, is a tantalizing way to enjoy the sweet orange-fleshed gourd. The addition of turmeric heightens the color as well as the flavor.

ROASTED BUTTERNUT SQUASH SOUP with GINGER

MAKES 8 TO 10 SERVINGS

1 large butternut squash (about 3 pounds), peeled, seeded, and cut into ¾-inch pieces

2 tablespoons extra-virgin olive oil

2 tablespoons pure maple syrup

2 tablespoons coconut oil

1 large yellow onion, chopped

2 medium carrots, chopped

2 tablespoons peeled and finely chopped fresh ginger

4 garlic cloves, minced

½ teaspoon ground turmeric

Sea salt and freshly ground black pepper

Position a rack in the center of the oven and preheat the oven to 400°F.

Toss the squash, olive oil, and maple syrup in a large bowl and spread it in a 10 by 15-inch baking dish. Bake, stirring occasionally, until the squash is tender, but not particularly browned, about 45 minutes.

Melt the coconut oil in a large saucepan. Add the onion, carrots, ginger, and garlic. Cook, stirring occasionally, until the onion is translucent, about 4 minutes. Stir in the roasted squash with its juices and the turmeric. Add enough cold water (about 8 cups) to just cover the squash, and bring it to a boil over high heat. Reduce the heat to medium-low and simmer until the carrots are very tender, about 20 minutes. Using an immersion blender, purée the soup. (To use a standing blender, let the soup cool until tepid. In batches, with the blender lid ajar, purée the soup and transfer to a bowl. Reheat the soup in the saucepan until piping hot.) Season to taste with salt and pepper and serve.

TOMATOES *have been shown to help prevent heart disease and reduce cancer rates due to their powerful antioxidants like vitamins C and E, beta-carotene, and numerous phytochemicals, including lycopene, lutein, and rutin. Cook your tomatoes in olive oil to enhance absorption of these health-promoting nutrients.* **—MEHMET**

This vegan soup is Zoe's absolute favorite meal. She's been known to eat it for breakfast, lunch, and dinner on the same day. It's delicately spiced and has a thick, velvety consistency, which makes it particularly satisfying on a brisk autumn afternoon.

"CREAMY" RED LENTIL, SWEET POTATO, and TOMATO SOUP

MAKES 10 TO 12 SERVINGS

2 tablespoons coconut oil

1 large yellow onion, chopped

1 medium red bell pepper, cored and cut into ½-inch dice

2 garlic cloves, minced

2 tablespoons cumin seeds, toasted and ground (see Note)

1 pound red lentils (2½ cups), picked over for stones, rinsed, and drained

One 28-ounce can crushed tomatoes

Fine sea salt and freshly ground black pepper

2 medium orange-fleshed sweet potatoes (about 1 pound), peeled and cut into ¾-inch cubes

One 14-ounce can coconut milk

Melt the oil in a large saucepan over medium heat. Add the onion, bell pepper, and garlic and cook, stirring occasionally, until the onion is tender but not browned, about 4 minutes. Add the cumin and stir well.

Add 8 cups water with the lentils, tomatoes, 1 teaspoon salt, and ½ teaspoon pepper. Bring to a simmer. Stir in the sweet potatoes, being sure they are submerged. Reduce the heat to medium-low and simmer, uncovered, stirring occasionally, until the lentils and sweet potatoes are tender, about 45 minutes. While the soup cooks, add hot water as needed to keep the sweet potatoes covered and prevent the soup from becoming too thick. During the last few minutes, stir in the coconut milk and heat it without boiling. Season to taste with salt and pepper. Ladle the soup into bowls and serve.

NOTE To toast cumin seeds, heat a small skillet over medium heat. Add the cumin seeds and cook, stirring occasionally, until the cumin is toasted and fragrant (you may see a whiff of smoke), about 2 minutes. Transfer the seeds to a plate and let cool completely before grinding in a coffee grinder or with a mortar and pestle. The seeds can also be crushed under a heavy skillet or saucepan on a work surface.

On the Island, it's called "Pasta Fa Zool." At least that's what my relatives call this hearty, tomato-based soup. I purée half of it to give it a thick, rich consistency, but it still has plenty of beans and ditalini floating around so you have something you can really sink your teeth into.

STATEN ISLAND PASTA E FAGIOLE

MAKES 6 TO 8 SERVINGS

2 tablespoons extra-virgin olive oil

½ large sweet onion, chopped

1 medium carrot, cut into ½-inch dice

1 medium celery rib, cut into ½-inch dice

2 garlic cloves, minced

1 teaspoon dried oregano

One 28-ounce can crushed tomatoes

Two 15-ounce cans cannellini (white kidney beans), drained and rinsed

2 dried bay leaves

Fine sea salt

Red pepper flakes

1½ cups ditalini or other short pasta for soup

Freshly grated pecorino romano cheese, for serving

Heat the oil in a large saucepan over medium heat. Add the onion, carrot, celery, and garlic. Cook, stirring occasionally, until the onion is translucent, about 5 minutes. Add the oregano and stir well.

Stir in 6 cups water along with the tomatoes, beans, bay leaves, ½ teaspoon salt, and ¼ teaspoon red pepper flakes. Bring to a boil over high heat. Reduce the heat to medium-low. Simmer the soup until the vegetables are tender, about 45 minutes.

Add the ditalini and bring to a boil over high heat. Return the heat to medium-low and simmer, stirring occasionally, until the pasta is very tender, adding hot water if needed, 15 to 20 minutes.

Discard the bay leaves. Transfer about half of the soup to a blender, set the lid ajar to allow the steam to escape, and purée the soup. Stir the puréed soup back into the remaining soup in the saucepan to thicken it. Season the soup to taste with additional salt and red pepper flakes.

Serve the soup with the romano passed on the side.

CANNELLINI (WHITE KIDNEY BEANS) are high in fiber and help reduce blood sugar. And relax about the gas. The more beans you eat, the more your body will build up the good bacteria you need to digest them. **—MEHMET**

On cold winter evenings there's nothing better than a big bowl of this hearty chili. The crumbled tofu gives it a robust consistency that even meat-eaters will love. Serve it over a bed of quinoa, or use brown rice instead—or skip the grain altogether and eat it like a chunky stew.

CHUNKY VEGETARIAN CHILI with QUINOA

MAKES 8 SERVINGS

CHILI

2 tablespoons extra-virgin olive oil

1 large sweet onion, chopped

2 medium carrots, cut into 1/2-inch dice

2 medium celery ribs, cut into 1/2-inch dice

1 jalapeño, seeded and minced

4 garlic cloves, minced

2 tablespoons chili powder

2 teaspoons ground cumin

2 teaspoons dried oregano

One 28-ounce can crushed tomatoes

One 12-ounce bottle lager beer

2 tablespoons pure maple syrup

1 canned chipotle chile in adobo, minced

One 15-ounce can kidney beans, drained and rinsed

One 15-ounce can black beans, drained and rinsed

Fine sea salt and freshly ground black pepper

CHILI TOFU

1 teaspoon extra-virgin olive oil

7 ounces extra-firm tofu, pressed (see Note, page 50) and crumbled

1 teaspoon chili powder

1 teaspoon ground cumin

1 teaspoon garlic powder

1/2 teaspoon fine sea salt

QUINOA

2 cups quinoa (use any color or the rainbow mix)

1 teaspoon fine sea salt

Chopped fresh cilantro, for garnish

Make the chili: Heat the oil in a large pot over medium heat. Add the onion, carrots, celery, jalapeño, and garlic and cook, stirring occasionally, until the onion is tender, about 10 minutes. Add the chili powder, cumin, and oregano and stir. Add the tomatoes, beer, 1 cup water, maple syrup, and chipotle and stir well. Bring to a simmer over high heat. Reduce the heat to medium-low and simmer, uncovered, until the vegetables are just tender, about 30 minutes. Stir in the kidney and black beans and cook for 10 minutes more.

(recipe continues)

Make the chili tofu: Heat the oil in a medium skillet over medium heat. Add the tofu and cook, until lightly browned, about 3 minutes. Combine the chili powder, cumin, garlic powder, and salt in a bowl. Sprinkle the chili mixture over the tofu and stir well. Stir the chili tofu into the chili and cook until it has thickened, about 10 minutes. Season to taste with the salt and pepper.

Make the quinoa: Place the quinoa in a fine-mesh wire sieve and rinse it well under cold water. (Don't skip this step.) Drain well. Bring the drained quinoa, 2½ cups water, and the salt to a boil in a medium saucepan over high heat. Reduce the heat to medium-low. Cover and simmer until the quinoa is tender and has absorbed the liquid, 15 to 20 minutes. Remove from the stove and let stand for 5 minutes. Fluff the quinoa with a fork. Spoon the quinoa into wide soup bowls and top with the chili. Sprinkle with the cilantro and serve.

The "meatiness" of a fresh portobello mushroom makes it a superb burger substitute. And though it works just fine with the traditional "lettuce and tomato thing," I think arugula and red pepper provide a bolder taste.

GRILLED PORTOBELLO BURGER with MARINATED ONION and WASABI MAYONNAISE

MAKES 4 SERVINGS

MARINATED ONION

3 tablespoons fresh lime juice

1 tablespoon honey

1/4 teaspoon fine sea salt

1/2 large sweet onion, cut into thin half-moons

MARINATED MUSHROOMS

4 fresh portobello mushroom caps

Vegetable Marinade (page 279)

WASABI MAYONNAISE

2 teaspoons rice vinegar (not seasoned rice vinegar)

1 1/2 teaspoons wasabi powder

1/2 cup vegetarian or standard mayonnaise

4 whole wheat sandwich buns, split open

1 red bell pepper, roasted (see Note, page 80), peeled, seeded, and cut into 1/2-inch strips

1 cup baby arugula

To marinate the onion: Whisk the lime juice, honey, and salt together in a medium bowl. Add the onion and mix to combine. Let stand for at least 30 minutes and up to 2 hours.

To marinate the mushrooms: Put the mushroom caps in a shallow glass or ceramic baking dish large enough to hold them in a single layer. Pour in the marinade. Turn the mushrooms to coat with the marinade and let stand for 30 minutes and up to 2 hours.

(recipe continues)

NOTE To roast a bell pepper, prepare an outdoor grill for direct cooking over high (500°F or higher) heat. Do not oil the pepper or the grill grates. Put the pepper on the grill, and close the lid. Cook, with the lid closed as much as possible, turning occasionally, until the skin is blackened and blistered, 10 to 15 minutes. Transfer the pepper to a bowl and cover the bowl with a plate. Let stand until the pepper cools, about 15 minutes. Remove the skin, seeds, ribs, and stem.

To make the mayonnaise: Whisk the vinegar and wasabi together in a small bowl. Add the mayonnaise and mix well. Cover the bowl with plastic wrap and let the mayonnaise stand for at least 30 minutes and up to 2 hours.

Prepare an outdoor grill for direct cooking over medium (400°F) heat.

Remove the mushrooms from the marinade and shake off the excess marinade. Place the mushrooms on the cooking grate and cover the grill. Cook with the lid closed, flipping the mushrooms once or twice, until the mushrooms are heated through, about 6 minutes. Transfer the mushrooms to a plate. Add the buns to the grill and cook, turning once, until hot, about 1 minute. Transfer the buns to a second plate.

Spread each of the buns with about 2 tablespoons of the mayonnaise. Add a grilled mushroom cap and top with one-quarter each of the onion, bell pepper, and arugula. Serve immediately.

LIMES are loaded with vitamin C, which is beneficial in helping the liver get rid of toxins. They also contain a natural flavonoid called hesperidin that has been shown to help combat breast, colon, lung, and liver cancer.
—MEHMET

ONIONS *are full of polyphenols like quercetin, which helps protect our cells from oxidative stress. They also contain high levels of folate, which improves mood, sleep, and appetite.* **—MEHMET**

In this sandwich, thyme-scented squash provides an excellent counterpoint to the barnyardy (yes, that's a real word) flavor of goat cheese. I love to serve it with a kale salad for a weekend lunch.

OPEN-FACED BUTTERNUT SQUASH and GOAT CHEESE SANDWICH

MAKES 4 SERVINGS

ROASTED SQUASH

1 medium butternut squash (about 2½ pounds), peeled, seeded, and cut into ¾-inch pieces

2 tablespoons extra-virgin olive oil

1 tablespoon pure maple syrup

1 teaspoon finely chopped fresh thyme, plus more for serving

2 garlic cloves, chopped

CARAMELIZED ONION

1 tablespoon extra-virgin olive oil

1 large sweet onion, cut into thin half-moons

Fine sea salt and freshly ground black pepper

4 slices sprouted wheat bread, toasted

1 cup crumbled goat cheese

To make the squash: Preheat the oven to 425°F. Toss the squash, oil, maple syrup, thyme, and garlic together in a large bowl. Spread the mixture in a 10 by 15-inch glass or ceramic baking dish. Bake, stirring occasionally, until the squash is tender, about 40 minutes.

To make the onion: Heat the oil in a large skillet over medium heat. Add the onion and cover the skillet. Cook, stirring occasionally, until the onion softens, about 5 minutes. Uncover and cook, stirring occasionally, until the onion is very tender and golden brown, about 25 minutes. Season to taste with salt and pepper. Remove from the heat and cover with the skillet lid ajar to keep warm.

Transfer the squash mixture with any juices to a medium bowl. Mash well with a potato masher or large fork into a chunky purée. If the mixture is dry, add a few tablespoons of water until it is moist and spreadable. (Whether you need water or not depends on the moisture content of the squash.) Season to taste with salt and pepper.

Spread each toast with an equal amount of the mashed squash, and top with ¼ cup goat cheese. Add as much onion as you wish (any remaining onion can be saved for another use), sprinkle with more thyme, and serve.

My mom made up this recipe when I was in high school and our family was just venturing into the world of vegetarian cooking. It's a delicious vegan alternative to tuna or egg salad.

CURRIED CHICKPEA SPREAD SANDWICH

MAKES 4 SANDWICHES

SALAD

Two 15-ounce cans chickpeas (garbanzo beans), drained and rinsed

1 medium celery rib, finely chopped

2 tablespoons finely chopped shallots

2 tablespoons finely chopped fresh flat-leaf parsley

½ cup vegetarian or standard mayonnaise

1 tablespoon red wine vinegar

1 teaspoon curry powder

½ teaspoon ground turmeric

Fine sea salt and freshly ground black pepper

1 cup chopped romaine lettuce

1 large ripe tomato, seeded and cut into ½-inch dice

4 whole wheat pitas, tops cut off

To make the salad: Coarsely mash the chickpeas, celery, shallots, and parsley together with a potato masher or large fork in a medium bowl. Be careful not to overdo it or the chickpeas will become mushy. Add the mayonnaise, vinegar, curry powder, and turmeric and mix well. Season to taste with the salt and pepper. (The salad can be covered and refrigerated for up to 3 days.)

Divide the salad, the lettuce, and tomato equally among the pitas and serve.

This sandwich was inspired by the flavors of the Mediterranean: the crunch of cucumber, the salty bite of Kalamata olives, the light char on the grilled eggplant, topped with an unctuous drizzle of tahini dressing. One bite and you'll feel transported to a Greek isle.

MEDITERRANEAN GRILLED EGGPLANT WRAP

MAKES 4 WRAPS

2 moderately small eggplants, such as graffiti or Japanese (about 8 ounces each), cut crosswise into 1/8-inch slices

Fine sea salt

Vegetable Marinade (page 279)

TAHINI DRESSING

3 tablespoons tahini

3 tablespoons fresh lemon juice

1 tablespoon extra-virgin olive oil

1 teaspoon honey

1 teaspoon ground cumin

2 garlic cloves, crushed through a press

1/4 teaspoon red pepper flakes

Fine sea salt

Four 6-inch whole-grain tortillas

4 tablespoons store-bought hummus

1 cup crumbled feta cheese (4 ounces)

2 Persian or Israeli cucumbers, cut into thin rounds

2 ripe plum (Roma) tomatoes, seeded and cut into 1/2-inch dice

1/2 cup pitted and coarsely chopped black olives, preferably Kalamata

Red pepper flakes

Sprinkle the eggplant slices on both sides with salt. Let the eggplant drain on paper towels to extract the bitter juices, about 30 minutes. Rinse the eggplant quickly under cold running water and pat dry with paper towels.

Arrange the eggplant, overlapping as needed, in a shallow glass or ceramic baking dish. Pour in the marinade. Turn the eggplant to coat with the marinade and let stand at room temperature for 30 minutes.

To make the dressing: Whisk all of the ingredients with 3 tablespoons water in a small bowl. Set aside.

(recipe continues)

Prepare an outdoor grill for direct cooking over medium heat (400°F).

Remove the eggplant from the marinade and shake off the excess marinade. Place the eggplant on the cooking grate, with the eggplant perpendicular to the grill grid, and cover the grill. Cook, with the lid closed as much as possible, flipping the eggplant once or twice, until the eggplant is tender, about 6 minutes. Transfer the eggplant to a plate. Add the tortillas to the grill and cook, turning once, until hot, about 1 minute. Transfer the tortillas to a second plate.

For each wrap, spread a warm tortilla with 1 tablespoon hummus. Top with one-quarter each of the feta cheese, grilled eggplant, the cucumber rounds, diced tomatoes, and olives. Drizzle with about 1 tablespoon of the tahini dressing and sprinkle with red pepper flakes to taste. Roll up the wrap and serve. (Any remaining dressing can be covered and refrigerated for up to 1 week to use as a salad dressing.)

TAHINI contains the essential minerals zinc, magnesium, and calcium. Zinc protects against infection and promotes wound healing and reproductive health. Magnesium is vital for nerve function, muscle contraction, and optimal immune function. And calcium, as we all know, is vital for healthy bones but also for blood clotting and regulating heart function. —MEHMET

Recently, one of my kids asked me if I missed eating meat. I don't, but if I did, it would only be bacon. There's something so alluring about the smoky, salty little strips. When I make this sandwich I use a tempeh version, but I'll understand if you go for the real thing.

BACON and AVOCADO SANDWICH with HORSERADISH MAYONNAISE

MAKES 4 SANDWICHES

HORSERADISH MAYONNAISE

½ cup mayonnaise

1 tablespoon drained prepared horseradish

1 teaspoon white wine vinegar

½ teaspoon honey

¼ teaspoon cayenne pepper

12 slices bacon of your choice (tempeh, tofu, turkey, or pork)

8 slices sprouted wheat bread

1 large ripe beefsteak tomato, sliced

2 ripe Hass avocados, pitted, peeled, and sliced

Fine sea salt and freshly ground black pepper

2 romaine lettuce leaves, cut in half crosswise

To make the mayonnaise: Mix all of the ingredients in a small bowl. Cover and refrigerate while making the rest of the sandwich.

Position a rack in the center of the oven and preheat the oven to 400°F. Arrange the bacon in a single layer in a large rimmed baking sheet. The slices can overlap slightly, as they will shrink during cooking. Bake until the bacon is crisp and brown, 15 to 20 minutes. Transfer the bacon to paper towels to drain. Reduce the oven temperature to 200°F.

Toast the bread in a toaster and keep the toast warm in the oven.

Spread the mayonnaise on the toast. Place four pieces of the toast, mayonnaise side up, on the work surface. Divide the bacon, tomato, and avocado equally among the four bread slices. Season to taste with salt and pepper. Top each with a lettuce leaf half and a bread slice, mayonnaise side down. Cut each sandwich in half and serve.

Arabella and I love really spicy food—generally, the hotter the better. But sometimes we need to tone it down just a bit to let the other flavors in the dish come through. Case in point: this sandwich. Traditional hot sauce could overpower the delicate, smoky taste of the grilled vegetables, but green chile powder just helps to brighten them.

GRILLED SUMMER SQUASH and ONION SANDWICH with GREEN CHILE MAYONNAISE

MAKES 4 SANDWICHES

GREEN CHILE MAYONNAISE

1/3 cup vegetarian or standard mayonnaise

2 tablespoons finely chopped fresh chives

2 teaspoons pure green chile powder (see Note)

MARINATED SQUASH

1 large zucchini (about 9 ounces), cut lengthwise into 1/8-inch slices

1 large yellow summer squash (about 9 ounces), cut lengthwise into 1/8-inch slices

Vegetable Marinade (page 279)

GRILLED ONION

1 medium yellow onion, cut into 1/4-inch half-moons

1 tablespoon extra-virgin olive oil

Fine sea salt and freshly ground black pepper

4 pieces of focaccia, each 6 by 4 inches, split horizontally

4 ounces Monterey jack cheese, thinly sliced

1/2 cup halved cherry tomatoes

1/2 cup packed baby arugula

Fine sea salt and freshly ground black pepper

To make the mayonnaise: At least 2 hours before serving, stir the mayonnaise, chives, and green chile powder together in a small bowl. Cover with plastic wrap and refrigerate to combine the flavors, at least 2 and up to 24 hours.

(recipe continues)

NOTE Green chile powder is available at www.amazon.com and www.newmexicochile andristra.com. It is often made from Hatch chiles, known for their balanced heat, before they turn red. Buy a brand that is pure ground chile without any herbs, spices, or salt. (I also like green chile salt for seasoning things like eggs and vegetables with a single shake.)

To marinate the squash: Arrange the zucchini and summer squash, overlapping as needed, in a shallow glass or ceramic baking dish. Pour in the marinade. Turn the squash to coat with the marinade and let stand at room temperature for 30 minutes.

Prepare an outdoor grill for direct cooking over medium heat (400°F).

To prepare the onion: Toss the onion and oil in a medium bowl to coat. Season to taste with salt and pepper.

Place a perforated grilling tray on one side of the grill. Heap the onion slices on the grilling tray and close the grill. Cook, with the lid closed as much as possible, until the onion softens, about 6 minutes.

Remove the squash from the marinade and shake off the excess marinade. Place the squash on the cooking grate, with the squash perpendicular to the grate grid, and cover the grill. Cook, with the lid closed as much as possible, flipping the squash once or twice, and occasionally stirring the onion, until the squash is tender and the onion is softened and lightly browned, about 6 minutes more. Transfer the vegetables to a platter. Add the focaccia to the grill, cut sides down, and toast for about 1 minute. Transfer the focaccia to the platter.

Spread the cut sides of the focaccia with the green chile mayonnaise. Divide the squash and onion among the focaccia bottoms. Top each with one-fourth of the cheese (it will melt slightly from the heat of the vegetables). Divide the tomatoes and arugula among the sandwiches and season lightly with the salt and pepper. Cover each with a focaccia top, cut side down, and serve.

When my mom was eighteen, she spent several months training with the Mexican Olympic equestrian team. She returned with a love of the country and its cuisine, which she regularly expressed in Mexican-themed dinners. (Just about every birthday in our home was celebrated as a taco party.) With six kids in the kitchen, tacos can become a bit unmanageable, so she devised this technique of mixing the toppings together. It makes assembly much easier; and since it allows the flavors to meld, it actually tastes better, too.

VEGETARIAN REFRIED BEAN and SALSA TACOS

MAKES 4 TO 6 SERVINGS

REFRIED BEAN FILLING

1 tablespoon extra-virgin olive oil

1 small yellow onion, finely chopped

2 garlic cloves, minced

1 jalapeño, seeded and minced (optional)

2 teaspoons chili powder

2 teaspoons ground cumin

2 tablespoons tomato paste

Two 15-ounce cans vegetarian refried beans

ALL-IN-ONE SALSA

1 romaine lettuce heart, coarsely chopped

2 ripe medium tomatoes, seeded and cut into 1/2-inch dice

1/2 large sweet onion, chopped

One 6.75-ounce jar pimiento-stuffed green olives, drained and chopped (1 cup)

12 crisp corn taco shells

2 cups (8 ounces) shredded sharp Cheddar cheese

Chopped fresh cilantro, for serving

To make the filling: Heat the oil in a medium skillet over medium heat. Add the onion, garlic, and jalapeño, if using, and cook, stirring occasionally, until the onion is translucent, about 4 minutes. Add the chili powder and cumin and stir well. Add 3/4 cup water and the tomato

(recipe continues)

paste and stir to dissolve the paste. Add the beans and mix well. Cook, stirring often, until the beans are hot and spreadable, about 5 minutes.

To make the salsa: Mix the lettuce, tomatoes, sweet onion, and olives in a medium bowl.

Fill each taco shell about one-third of the way with the beans, cover with a thin layer of cheese so it will melt from the warmth of the beans, then top with a generous helping of the salsa. Serve with cilantro on the side.

SUNFLOWER SEEDS are a rich source of selenium, which helps reduce cell damage and prevent some cancers. They are also great for skin because of their high vitamin E content. —**MEHMET**

This sandwich tastes like the '70s to me. It's got that bean sprout/pita/sunflower seed groove that just kinda makes you want to wear tie-dyed bellbottoms. Try it and see if you can feel the love.

CALIFORNIA CUISINE VEGETARIAN PITA

MAKES 4 SANDWICHES

ITALIAN DRESSING

3 tablespoons red wine vinegar

1 teaspoon dried oregano

1 teaspoon honey

1 garlic clove, crushed through a press

1/2 cup extra virgin olive oil

Fine sea salt and freshly ground black pepper

4 whole wheat pitas, cut in half crosswise

1 ripe Hass avocado, sliced

4 button mushrooms, thinly sliced

1 large carrot, coarsely shredded

4 sweet pickled cherry peppers, drained and sliced (see Note)

8 teaspoons hulled sunflower seeds

1 cup alfalfa sprouts or baby arugula

Fine sea salt and freshly ground black pepper

To make the dressing: Whisk the vinegar, oregano, honey, and garlic in a small bowl. Gradually whisk in the oil. Season to taste with salt and pepper.

Open the halved pitas into pockets. Divide the avocado, mushrooms, carrot, and cherry peppers equally among the pita halves. Sprinkle 2 teaspoons sunflower seeds into each pita half. Add the alfalfa sprouts and season with salt and pepper. Drizzle a generous tablespoon of the dressing into each pita half and serve, with the remaining dressing passed on the side.

NOTE Pickled cherry peppers are beloved by Italian American cooks, and they are commonly sold at our local supermarkets and Italian delicatessens. Any sweet pickled red pepper is an acceptable substitute.

They say necessity is the mother of invention, and it certainly was in this case. The extended family was in Maine, celebrating the Fourth of July with a giant picnic. Preparations were going well until, at the last minute, someone noticed that we had no mayonnaise for the homemade lobster rolls. What we did have was avocados—lots of them. When thoroughly mashed, they had a luscious consistency that turned out to be way better than plain old mayo. Who knew?

GUAC-LOBSTER ROLLS

MAKES 4 SERVINGS

4 cooked lobsters
(see Note)

2 ripe Hass avocados,
coarsely chopped

2 tablespoons finely
chopped fresh chives

1 tablespoon fresh lime
juice

Fine sea salt and freshly
ground black pepper

4 hot dog buns,
preferably top-split

Softened butter, for
serving

Crack the lobsters and remove the shells of the tails, claws, and knuckles. (Don't bother cracking the small parts of the lobster.) Coarsely chop the lobster meat and pat it dry with paper towels.

Using a dinner fork, mash the avocados, chives, and lime juice together in a medium bowl. Add the lobster meat and mix well. Season to taste with salt and pepper.

Open the buns and toast them in a wide-slot toaster or under a hot broiler. Spread the insides of the buns lightly with butter. Fill each bun with an equal amount of the lobster mixture and serve immediately.

NOTE To cook the lobster at home, add enough salted water to fill a stockpot about two-thirds full, cover, and bring to a full boil over high heat. One at a time, add the lobsters to the pot and cover the pot again. Cook until the lobsters' shells turn an even red color, about 10 minutes. Using tongs, remove the lobsters from the pot and rinse well under cold running water. Transfer the lobsters to a large bowl of iced water and let cool.

SALADS

My sister Emily came up with this sweet and spicy fruit salad. On first glance you may be intimidated by the addition of both Sriracha and jalapeño, but don't be. They are cooled by the watermelon and cheese, and they give the dish just the right amount of piquancy.

SPICY WATERMELON SALAD
with FETA CHEESE

MAKES 4 TO 6 SERVINGS

SPICY VINAIGRETTE

1 tablespoon champagne or white wine vinegar

1 tablespoon extra-virgin olive oil

1 teaspoon honey

½ teaspoon seeded and minced jalapeño

½ teaspoon Sriracha or other Asian chili sauce

¼ teaspoon fine sea salt

¼ cup finely chopped fresh chives

¼ cold ripe seedless watermelon, cut into 1-inch chunks (about 7 cups)

4 ounces goat cheese, crumbled (1 cup)

To make the vinaigrette: Whisk the vinegar, oil, honey, jalapeño, Sriracha, and salt together in a small bowl to dissolve the honey. Stir in the chives.

Toss the watermelon and dressing together in a bowl. Sprinkle with the goat cheese and serve chilled.

WATERMELON is a potent immune-boosting food, rich in vitamins A and C. But it also contains high levels of glutathione, one of the most powerful detoxifying antioxidant molecules. —MEHMET

Egg salad is one of those classically underappreciated foods—at least in our home. It's not fancy. It's not exotic. It's been around forever. We tend to forget all about it—until one day (usually right after Easter) when, with one bite, we rediscover how amazing it actually is.

JALAPEÑO EGG SALAD
on LETTUCE LEAVES

MAKES 4 SERVINGS

EGG SALAD

6 large eggs

¼ cup mayonnaise

1 medium celery rib, finely chopped

1 tablespoon minced shallots

1 teaspoon Dijon mustard

1 teaspoon cider vinegar

1 teaspoon dried oregano

1 jalapeño, seeded and minced

Fine sea salt

Hot pepper sauce

12 small romaine heart leaves

To make the egg salad: Put the eggs in a single layer in a medium saucepan. Add enough cold water to cover the eggs by 1 inch. Bring the water to a boil over high heat. Remove the saucepan from the heat and cover it tightly. Let the eggs stand in the water for 15 minutes. Carefully drain the eggs and rinse them under cold water. Add them to a medium bowl of iced water. Let the eggs stand until they are completely chilled, about 15 minutes. Crack and peel the eggs under a thin stream of cold running water.

Chop the hard-boiled eggs into ½ inch dice. Transfer them to a medium bowl and add the mayonnaise, celery, shallots, mustard, vinegar, oregano, and jalapeño. Mix well and season to taste with salt and hot pepper sauce. (The egg salad can be covered and refrigerated for up to 2 days.)

Divide the salad evenly among the lettuce leaves, spooning the salad on the sturdier rib end of each leaf. Serve immediately.

Arugula is the Oz family's favorite leafy green. (Not that we don't love you, kale!) There's something about the sharp, peppery flavor that just seems to wake up a salad. Here we combine arugula with a tart burst from fresh pomegranate seeds and the delicate umami of goat cheese. The sweet pomegranate molasses in the dressing rounds it out for a perfectly balanced dish.

ARUGULA, GOAT CHEESE, and POMEGRANATE SALAD

MAKES 4 SERVINGS

DRESSING

1 tablespoon balsamic vinegar

1 tablespoon fresh lemon juice

1 teaspoon pomegranate molasses (see Note)

1 small garlic clove, crushed through a garlic press

2 tablespoons extra-virgin olive oil

Fine sea salt and freshly ground black pepper

5 ounces baby arugula (6 lightly packed cups)

½ cup chopped walnuts

⅓ cup pomegranate arils (seeds; see Note)

¾ cup crumbled goat cheese (3 ounces)

To make the dressing: Whisk the vinegar, lemon juice, pomegranate molasses, and garlic together in a small bowl. Gradually whisk in the oil. Season to taste with salt and pepper.

Toss the arugula, walnuts, and pomegranate arils together in a large bowl. Add the dressing and toss again. Sprinkle with the goat cheese and serve.

NOTE Pomegranate molasses is available at Mediterranean grocers and online. To remove the pomegranate arils from the fruit, fill a large bowl with cold water. Score the fruit into quarters, being sure not to cut into the juicy arils. Submerge the pomegranate in the water. Break the submerged pomegranate into quarters. Using your fingers, coax the arils out of the bitter white membrane—the arils will sink to the bottom of the bowl while any bits of membrane will float on the water. Skim off the membrane from the water and discard it and drain the arils.

ARUGULA is a cruciferous vegetable like cabbage, broccoli, and cauliflower. This dark leafy green contains the powerful antioxidant alpha-lipoic acid, which helps to combat free radicals, and indole-3-carbinol, which reduces inflammation. —MEHMET

This fiesta in a bowl is definitely more of a whole meal than a side salad. You can include an "add-in" if you like, but there's plenty of protein with the beans and cheese.

MEXICAN CHOPPED SALAD
with CREAMY CHIPOTLE DRESSING

MAKES 4 SERVINGS

DRESSING

1/2 cup vegetarian or standard mayonnaise

1/4 cup extra-virgin olive oil

2 tablespoons fresh lime juice

2 tablespoons finely chopped fresh chives

1 tablespoon balsamic vinegar

1/2 canned chipotle chile in adobo, including seeds, minced

1/2 teaspoon granulated garlic or garlic powder

Fine sea salt

SALAD

2 romaine lettuce hearts (about 7 ounces each), coarsely chopped

One 15-ounce can black beans, drained and rinsed

1 1/2 cups cooked corn kernels, cut from about 2 ears boiled or grilled corn

2 ripe Hass avocados, cut into 3/4-inch dice

1 large ripe tomato, cut into 3/4-inch dice

1/2 cup shredded sharp Cheddar cheese (2 ounces)

2 scallions (white and green parts), thinly sliced

To make the dressing: Whisk the mayonnaise, oil, lime juice, chives, balsamic vinegar, chipotle, and granulated garlic together in a small bowl, seasoning to taste with the salt. Set the dressing aside.

To make the salad: Toss the lettuce, black beans, corn, avocados, tomato, Cheddar, and scallions in a large bowl.

Serve the salad in individual bowls and pass the dressing on the side.

AVOCADOS are a wonderful source of monounsaturated fats (MUFAS), which help reduce inflammation in the body. They also contain biotin, which keeps your skin moist and supple. —**MEHMET**

This salad is a study in contrasts: the clean snap of cucumber beside the soft caramelized flesh of melon, the coolness of mint against the jalapeño's heat, and the sharp pungency of chives with the tangy creaminess of goat cheese. We like to think of it as a culinary yin-yang symbol.

CUCUMBER and GRILLED CANTALOUPE SALAD

JALAPEÑO AND HERB
VINAIGRETTE

1 tablespoon white wine
vinegar

1/2 teaspoon seeded and
minced fresh jalapeño

1/2 cup extra-virgin
olive oil

1 tablespoon finely
chopped fresh mint

1 tablespoon finely
chopped fresh chives

Fine sea salt and freshly
ground black pepper

1/2 ripe cantaloupe,
seeded and cut into
3/4-inch unpeeled wedges

8 chilled Persian or Israeli
cucumbers, cut into thin
rounds

Fine sea salt and freshly
ground black pepper

1/2 cup crumbled goat
cheese (2 ounces)

Finely chopped fresh
chives, for garnish

Fresh mint sprigs, for
garnish

To make the vinaigrette: Whisk the vinegar and jalapeño together in a small bowl. Gradually whisk in the oil. Stir in the mint and chives, and season to taste with the salt and pepper.

Prepare an outdoor grill for direct cooking over medium heat (400°F).

Lightly brush the cantaloupe flesh with some of the vinaigrette. Place the cantaloupe on the grill, running perpendicular to the cooking grate. Grill, with the lid closed, flipping the cantaloupe over halfway through grilling, until the cantaloupe is seared with grill marks on both sides, about 4 minutes. Transfer the cantaloupe to a chopping board and let cool. Cut off and discard the cantaloupe skin, and cut the flesh into 1-inch-long pieces. Transfer the cantaloupe to a bowl, cover, and refrigerate until chilled, at least 1 hour.

Toss the cantaloupe, the cucumbers, and the vinaigrette together in a medium bowl. Season to taste with salt and pepper. Transfer the cucumber mixture to a platter. Sprinkle with the goat cheese, followed by the chives. Top with the mint sprigs and serve.

CUCUMBERS are full of unique polyphenols that benefit your skin, reduce your risk of cancer, and combat inflammation. They also kill the bacteria in your mouth that cause bad breath. —MEHMET

Where we live in New Jersey, pretty much every town has a Greek diner. While it may be tempting to order take-out, we prefer this homemade version of the ubiquitous Greek salad. (Plus, it takes less time than the delivery guy.)

GREEK SALAD with LEMON-GARLIC DRESSING

MAKES 4 TO 6 SERVINGS

MARINATED ONION

½ large sweet onion, thinly sliced

¼ teaspoon dried oregano

⅛ teaspoon fine sea salt

DRESSING

2 tablespoons red wine vinegar

2 tablespoons fresh lemon juice

1 teaspoon honey

¼ teaspoon dried oregano

2 garlic cloves, crushed through a garlic press

½ cup extra-virgin olive oil

Fine sea salt and freshly ground black pepper

SALAD

3 romaine hearts, torn into bite-size pieces

1 pint cherry tomatoes, halved

6 ounces drained feta cheese, cut into ½-inch slices

4 Persian or Israeli cucumbers, cut into ¼-inch slices

½ cup oil-cured black olives (not pitted), preferably Gaeta

6 pepperoncini (pickled Italian peppers), drained and cut into ¼-inch rings

2 tablespoons finely chopped fresh mint

2 tablespoons finely chopped fresh dill

To marinate the onion: Combine the onion, oregano, and salt in a medium bowl. Let stand for at least 30 minutes and up to 2 hours. Drain off the onion juices before serving.

To make the dressing: Whisk the vinegar, lemon juice, honey, oregano, and garlic to dissolve the honey. Gradually whisk in the oil. Season to taste with salt and pepper.

To make the salad: Put the romaine in a large bowl. Placing each ingredient in its own area, top with the marinated onion, the cherry tomatoes, feta cheese, cucumbers, olives, and pepperoncini. Sprinkle with the mint and dill. Present the salad to the table, showing its colors. Drizzle with the dressing, toss well, and serve.

This salad has a delicious sea-infused aroma without being too "fishy." Many health food stores or Asian markets carry marinated hijiki, though I usually buy it dried and prepare it at home. I love the tender mâche leaves as a base, but you can substitute another soft lettuce.

HIJIKI, MÂCHE, and EDAMAME SALAD

MAKES 4 TO 6 SERVINGS

MARINATED HIJIKI

Two 0.55-ounce packages hijiki

1 tablespoon tamari or soy sauce

1 tablespoon honey

2 teaspoons brown rice vinegar

MISO DRESSING

¼ cup white (shiro) miso

¼ cup brown rice vinegar

2 tablespoons mirin

1 garlic clove, minced

7 ounces mâche or other tender, mild salad greens

1½ cups frozen shelled edamame (8 ounces), cooked according to package directions

4 medium carrots, shredded

2 teaspoons sesame seeds

To marinate the hijiki: Put the hijiki in a medium bowl and add enough cold tap water to cover. Let stand for 10 minutes. Drain the hijiki, return to the bowl, cover with more water, and let stand until the hijiki is tender, about 10 minutes more. Drain the hijiki well.

Whisk the tamari, honey, and vinegar together in a medium bowl to dissolve the honey. Add the hijiki and mix well. Cover the bowl and refrigerate for at least 1 hour and up to 2 days.

To make the miso dressing: Whisk the miso, rice vinegar, mirin, and garlic together in a small bowl.

Toss the mâche, edamame, and dressing together in a medium serving bowl. Spread the shredded carrots over the top and place the marinated hijiki in a small mound in the center. Serve the salad, sprinkling each portion with about ½ teaspoon of the sesame seeds.

SEAWEED is famous for being high in iodine, an essential nutrient for thyroid function, but seaweed is also an excellent source of omega-3 fats. Hijiki varieties are super-rich in iron, so you will also have plenty of red blood cells to cart oxygen around your body. —**MEHMET**

We Ozes never tire of kale. In this scrumptious salad, we add it to farro, which has a mild nutty flavor, then toss it with almonds, apples, and pomegranate seeds to give it a sweet crunch.

SALAD with KALE, FARRO, and WINTER FRUITS

MAKES 6 SERVINGS

TOASTED ALMONDS

1/2 cup slivered almonds

1 tablespoon extra-virgin olive oil

1/2 teaspoon garlic salt

HERB VINAIGRETTE

2 tablespoons cider vinegar

1 1/2 teaspoons finely chopped fresh oregano

1 1/2 teaspoons finely chopped fresh thyme

1 teaspoon pure maple syrup

2 garlic cloves, crushed through a garlic press

1/3 cup plus 1 tablespoon extra-virgin olive oil

Fine sea salt and freshly ground black pepper

2 pounds kale, preferably lacinato (also called Tuscan or dinosaur)

1 tablespoon fresh lemon juice

Fine sea salt

2 cups Basic Farro (page 274), cooled

1 sweet apple, such as Honeycrisp, cored and cut into 1/2-inch slivers

1/2 cup pomegranate arils (seeds; see Note, page 104)

Freshly ground black pepper

To make the almonds: Position a rack in the center of the oven and preheat the oven to 350°F. Toss the almonds with the oil and garlic salt on a large rimmed baking sheet. Bake, stirring occasionally, until the almonds are lightly toasted, 10 to 12 minutes. Transfer the almonds to a plate and let them cool completely.

To make the vinaigrette: Whisk the vinegar, oregano, thyme, maple syrup, and garlic together in a small bowl. Gradually whisk in the oil. Season to taste with salt and pepper.

Tear off and discard the kale stems. In batches, submerge the kale in a sink or large bowl of cold water and agitate

(recipe continues)

the leaves well to remove any grit. Lift the kale out of the water and shake off the excess water. Stack the leaves and cut them crosswise into thin strips. Spin the kale dry in a salad spinner and transfer to a large bowl.

Drizzle the kale with the lemon juice and sprinkle with ½ teaspoon salt. Using your hands, rub and massage the kale well. (This helps to tenderize the kale.) Let the kale stand for 10 minutes.

Add the cooled almonds, the farro, apple, and pomegranate arils to the kale. Drizzle with the vinaigrette and toss well. Season to taste with salt and pepper and serve.

KALE America has fallen in love with this excellent source of vitamins A, C, and K. It is high in fiber, low in calories, and packed with phytonutrients like quercetin, lutein, and indole-3-carbinol. —MEHMET

Mehmet and I visited Thailand for the wedding of a close friend almost twenty years ago, and it has remained one of our favorite places on the planet. We fell in love with the people, the culture, and the sights, but mostly we were smitten with the food. This Thai-inspired salad has a nice tartness from the lime and ginger in the dressing, while the carrot and bean sprouts give it a great crunchy texture.

SALAD with PEANUT DRESSING

MAKES 4 TO 6 SERVINGS

PEANUT DRESSING

¼ cup smooth natural-style peanut butter

¼ cup fresh lime juice

2 tablespoons white wine vinegar

1 tablespoon pure maple syrup

1 teaspoon finely grated fresh ginger (use the small holes on a box grater)

1 garlic clove, minced

¼ teaspoon toasted sesame oil

½ cup extra-virgin olive oil

Fine sea salt

2 heads Boston lettuce, torn into bite-size pieces

3 cups loosely packed bean sprouts (6 ounces)

1 large carrot, shredded

2 scallions (white and green parts), finely chopped

Teriyaki Baked Tofu (page 272) or Sautéed Chicken Breast (page 270), or both

½ cup coarsely chopped peanuts

3 tablespoons coarsely chopped fresh cilantro

To make the dressing: Whisk the peanut butter, lime juice, vinegar, maple syrup, ginger, garlic, and sesame oil together with 2 tablespoons water in a small bowl. Gradually whisk in the olive oil. Season to taste with salt.

Toss the lettuce, bean sprouts, carrot, and scallions together in a large bowl. Add the dressing and toss again.

Divide the salad among individual bowls. Top each salad with equal amounts of the tofu, and sprinkle with the peanuts and cilantro. Serve immediately.

Daphne makes a giant bowl of this shredded cabbage salad whenever we have a lot of people coming for lunch. It's lighter than traditional coleslaw and pairs nicely with a variety of entrées, from burgers to grilled fish.

ASIAN SLAW with GINGER DRESSING

MAKES 4 TO 6 SERVINGS

GINGER DRESSING

One 2-inch piece fresh ginger, shredded on the large holes of a box grater

2 tablespoons fresh lime juice

1 tablespoon brown rice vinegar

1 teaspoon tamari or soy sauce

1 teaspoon pure maple syrup

1 garlic clove, crushed through a garlic press

¼ teaspoon toasted sesame oil

Pinch of cayenne pepper

¼ cup extra-virgin olive oil

1 small green cabbage (about 1½ pounds), cored and thinly shredded

4 medium carrots, shredded (1 cup)

4 scallions (white and green parts), thinly sliced

2 tablespoons finely chopped fresh cilantro

Kosher salt and freshly ground black pepper

½ cup coarsely chopped raw or roasted cashews

To make the dressing: Working over a bowl, squeeze the ginger to extract its juice. Measure 1 tablespoon of the juice and transfer to a small bowl. Add the lime juice, vinegar, tamari, maple syrup, garlic, sesame oil, and cayenne pepper and whisk to combine. Gradually whisk in the olive oil.

Combine the cabbage, carrots, scallions, and cilantro in a large bowl. Add the dressing and toss well. Season to taste with salt and pepper. Cover and refrigerate for 1 to 2 hours.

Sprinkle the cashews on top and serve chilled.

GINGER is a powerful digestive aid and helps to relieve nausea. Ginger is also used to reduce inflammation, thereby relieving headaches and arthritis. It has antiviral properties as well, which makes it a frequent remedy for the common cold. —**MEHMET**

On some evenings, when none of our schedules seem to coincide, I just put out my version of a salad bar and let everyone assemble his or her own dinner. I start with a big bowl of greens, then arrange a selection of toppings, being sure to include a protein or two. Often, there are leftovers in the refrigerator I can toss in as well, like Roasted Savory Vegetables (page 146) or Braised Beets (page 135).

OZ FAMILY SALAD BAR

MAKES 6 SERVINGS

8 ounces mixed baby greens

Oz Family House Dressing (page 281)

PROTEIN (CHOOSE ONE OR TWO)

Sautéed Chicken Breast (page 270)

Quick Shrimp with Garlic and Lemon (page 271)

Spiced Baked Chickpeas (page 273)

Teriyaki Baked Tofu (page 272)

NUTS AND SEEDS (CHOOSE ONE OR TWO)

1 cup coarsely chopped walnuts, slivered almonds, or pine nuts

1/2 cup hulled sunflower seeds, hemp seeds, or pumpkin seeds

CHEESE (CHOOSE ONE)

4 to 6 ounces goat, feta, or Gorgonzola cheese, crumbled (1 to 1 1/2 cups)

4 to 6 ounces sharp Cheddar cheese, shredded (1 1/2 cups)

DRIED AND FRESH FRUIT (CHOOSE ONE OR TWO)

1/2 cup dried tart cherries or dried cranberries

1/2 cup fresh pomegranate arils (seeds; see Note, page 104)

1 large navel orange, peeled and cut between membranes into segments

2 mandarin oranges, peeled and separated into segments

1 Granny Smith apple, cored and cut into bite-size pieces

Put out a large bowl of baby greens, a container with the vinaigrette, and bowls of your chosen protein, nuts, seeds, cheese, and fruit. Let the diners serve themselves.

VEGETABLES

This is what I order at Japanese restaurants when everyone else is getting sushi. Ideally, the eggplant will become butter-soft and the miso will form a sweet, caramelized glaze. Use a white (also called shiro) miso and small Japanese or graffiti eggplants for best results.

ROASTED EGGPLANT
with MISO GLAZE

MAKES 4 TO 6 SERVINGS

3 small eggplants, such as Japanese or graffiti (each about 8 ounces)

1 teaspoon fine sea salt

MISO GLAZE

⅓ cup white (shiro) miso

2 tablespoons fresh ginger juice (see Note)

1 tablespoon extra-virgin olive oil

1 tablespoon tamari or soy sauce

1 teaspoon mirin

1 teaspoon honey

Extra-virgin olive oil, for brushing

1 scallion (white and green parts), minced

2 teaspoons sesame seeds (optional)

Trim off and discard the eggplant stems. Cut the eggplants lengthwise into slices about ½ inch thick. Sprinkle the eggplant on both sides with the salt. Place the eggplant in a colander and let drain on a plate for 30 to 60 minutes.

To make the glaze: Whisk the miso, ginger juice, oil, tamari, mirin, and honey together in a small bowl.

Position a rack in the center of the oven and preheat to 400°F.

Heat a large ridged grill pan over medium heat. Pat the eggplant dry with paper towels. Brush the eggplant with the oil. Place the eggplant in the grill pan (you may do this in batches) and cook, turning once, until the eggplant is seared with grill marks and softened, but not cooked through, about 5 minutes. Transfer the eggplant to a large rimmed baking sheet.

Score two or three shallow (about ⅛ inch) lengthwise slits into each eggplant slice. Divide the glaze equally over the eggplant tops, spreading it evenly. Sprinkle the scallion over the eggplant slices. Bake until the eggplant is tender and the glaze is bubbling, 10 to 15 minutes. Sprinkle with the sesame seeds, if using, and serve.

NOTE For each tablespoon of ginger juice needed, estimate about 1 ounce of fresh ginger. Choose firm, juicy ginger with a tight and smooth skin—do not use wrinkled, old specimens. Shred the ginger (no need to peel) on the large holes of a box grater. In batches, working over a bowl, squeeze the shredded ginger in your fist to extract and collect the juice. (Or add the shredded ginger to a potato ricer and press firmly to remove the juice.)

EGGPLANT'S distinctive trait, the rich purple color, is created by bountiful flavonoids. In fact, many of the nutritional benefits gained from consuming eggplant are obtained from the skin of the vegetable, which is full of fiber, potassium, and magnesium, as well as antioxidants. Eggplants are also a "bulking agent" and satiate your appetite without the burden of too many calories. Your heart and waist will thank you as much as your taste buds.
—MEHMET

Daphne makes these pretty much every time she comes over, and the entire family hovers around the oven like vultures, waiting for them to be done. They get their captivating flavor from the tiny black nigella seeds sprinkled liberally over the top.

GLAZED ACORN SQUASH
with SAVORY SEEDS

MAKES 4 TO 6 SERVINGS

1 acorn squash (about 2 pounds)

2 tablespoons coconut oil, melted

1 tablespoon pure maple syrup

1 teaspoon cumin seeds

1 teaspoon nigella seeds

1 garlic clove, finely chopped

1 teaspoon fine sea salt

½ teaspoon red pepper flakes

Chopped fresh mint, for garnish

Position a rack in the center of the oven and preheat the oven to 400°F.

Cut the squash lengthwise into 12 equal wedges, discarding the seeds. Place the wedges, flat side down, on a large rimmed baking sheet. Mix the coconut oil, maple syrup, cumin seeds, nigella seeds, garlic, salt, and red pepper flakes together in a small bowl. Spoon the mixture on each wedge, using the back of the spoon to spread the mixture over the squash.

Bake until the squash is tender when pierced with the tip of a small sharp knife, 30 to 40 minutes. Transfer the squash to a platter, sprinkle with the mint, and serve.

The summer after Mehmet and I were engaged, I went to visit him in Turkey. I was awed by the country—its rich history, culture, and natural beauty. And the food was magnificent, at once both foreign and familiar, subtle and exciting. The dish I found most enticing was *imam bayildi*, or "the priest fainted." According to legend, the holy man who first tasted it took a single bite and became so ecstatic that he passed out. Try it and see if its exotic flavors make you swoon!

"THE PRIEST FAINTED" EGGPLANT

MAKES 4 SERVINGS

2 medium globe eggplants (about 1¼ pounds each)

Fine sea salt

¼ cup extra-virgin olive oil, plus more for brushing and serving

5 large garlic cloves, thinly sliced

2 medium yellow onions, chopped

Two 28-ounce cans plum tomatoes in juice, drained, tomatoes coarsely crushed by hand

¼ cup finely chopped fresh flat-leaf parsley, plus more for serving

4 teaspoons finely chopped fresh oregano

¼ teaspoon red pepper flakes

½ cup pine nuts, toasted (see Note, page 130)

½ cup plain Greek yogurt, for serving

Cut each eggplant in half lengthwise, leaving the top stems attached. (This keeps the filling from oozing out.) Using a soupspoon, scoop out the eggplant flesh, leaving a shell about ½ inch thick. Save the eggplant flesh for another use.

Season the insides of the shells with 1 teaspoon salt. Place the shells, cut side down, on a plate, and let drain for 30 to 45 minutes.

(recipe continues)

NOTE To toast pine nuts, heat a medium skillet over medium heat. Add the pine nuts and cook, stirring often, until they are toasted, about 2 minutes. Transfer them immediately to a plate and let them cool.

Position a rack in the top third of the oven and preheat the oven to 400°F.

Pat the eggplant shells dry with paper towels. Brush the cut sides with olive oil. Place the eggplants, cut sides up, in a baking dish. Bake until the eggplant is tender when pierced with the tip of a small sharp knife, about 45 minutes.

Meanwhile, heat the ¼ cup oil in a medium skillet over medium heat. Add the garlic and cook, stirring almost constantly, until it is softened but not browned, about 1 minute. Add the onions and mix well. Cook, stirring occasionally, until the onions are translucent but not browned, about 4 minutes. Stir in the tomatoes, parsley, oregano, and red pepper flakes, and bring the mixture to a simmer. Reduce the heat to medium-low and simmer, stirring occasionally, until slightly thickened, about 10 minutes. Stir in the pine nuts. Season to taste with salt.

Remove the baking dish with the eggplant from the oven. Divide the tomato mixture equally among the eggplant shells. Return to the oven and continue baking until the tomato filling is just beginning to brown, about 20 minutes. Remove the baking dish from the oven. Top each eggplant half with a large dollop of yogurt, a drizzle of oil, and a sprinkle of parsley. Cut each eggplant in half crosswise and serve.

OLIVE OIL is the foundation of the Mediterranean diet, which has the most data supporting its benefits for longevity. It is rich in antioxidant phenols, reduces inflammation, and lowers LDL (bad) cholesterol levels, though not HDL (good) cholesterol. —MEHMET

I love adding fruit and nuts to vegetable dishes. In this recipe, grilling adds a smoky undercurrent that unifies the tastes and textures.

GRILLED ASPARAGUS and PEACHES with CARAMELIZED SHALLOTS and HAZELNUTS

MAKES 4 SERVINGS

Extra-virgin olive oil

3 tablespoons coarsely chopped shallots

¼ cup toasted, skinned, and coarsely chopped hazelnuts (see Note, page 132)

Fine sea salt and freshly ground black pepper

2 pounds thin asparagus, woody stems snapped off and discarded

1 large firm-ripe freestone peach, cut into 12 wedges

Prepare an outdoor grill for direct cooking over medium (400°F) heat.

Heat 1 tablespoon of the oil in a medium skillet over medium-low heat. Add the shallots and cook, stirring often, until they are golden brown, about 5 minutes. Stir in the hazelnuts. Season the mixture with salt and pepper and remove from the heat.

Place the asparagus on a large rimmed baking sheet, drizzle with a tablespoon or two of oil, and roll them in the oil to coat them. Lightly brush the peach wedges with oil to coat them.

Place the asparagus on one side of the grill, perpendicular to the grill grid. Place the peaches, also running perpendicular to the grid, on the grill. Cover the grill and cook, occasionally rolling the asparagus to turn them and flipping the peaches once, until the asparagus is crisp-tender and the peaches have sear marks, about 6 minutes. Remove the asparagus and peaches from the grill. Season them to taste with salt and pepper.

Arrange the asparagus on a serving platter. Top with the peaches, followed by the hazelnut mixture, and serve.

NOTE Toasted and skinned hazelnuts are sometimes available at specialty markets. (Don't confuse these with the ones that are skinned, but not toasted, which can be detected by their very pale color.) If the hazelnuts still have their dark brown skins, you'll have to toast and skin them at home in a conventional oven or, if you find it more efficient for a small amount, a countertop toaster oven.

Spread the nuts on a rimmed baking sheet (or the toaster oven tray). Bake at 350°F, stirring occasionally, until the skins are curling and the nut flesh is lightly browned, 12 to 15 minutes. Let the hazelnuts cool until easy to handle, about 20 minutes. Wrap the hazelnuts in a kitchen towel, and use the towel to rub the nuts against one another to remove the skins. Don't worry about getting every last bit of the skins off.

ASPARAGUS has lots of vitamins C, E, and K, as well as folate for brain health and glutathione for detoxification. It also contains the trace mineral chromium, which helps metabolize carbohydrates and regulate blood sugar.
—MEHMET

BEETS *The nitrates in beets are converted to nitric oxide in the body and the nitric oxide improves blood flow by dilating the vessels. Beets also have iron, which helps the blood transport oxygen, and high amounts of boron, which is utilized in the production of human sex hormones. This may be why beets have traditionally been thought of as an aphrodisiac. They get their rich color from betaine, which helps the liver in Phase 2 detoxification.* **—MEHMET**

Mehmet was never a fan of beets. (He had eaten them in the middle school cafeteria and was less than impressed.) So the first time I served them he had to be coaxed into even taking a bite. Now they're one of his favorite vegetables—especially when seasoned with this combo of citrus, nuts, and shallots.

BRAISED BEETS with ORANGE and PECANS

MAKES 4 TO 6 SERVINGS

2 pounds medium beets (about 12), trimmed and scrubbed under cold running water

¼ cup extra-virgin olive oil

2 tablespoons finely chopped shallots

Finely grated zest of ½ orange

2 tablespoons fresh orange juice

2 tablespoons pure maple syrup

2 tablespoons champagne or white wine vinegar

¼ cup coarsely chopped pecans, plus more for garnish

2 tablespoons finely chopped fresh chives, plus more for garnish

Fine sea salt and freshly ground black pepper

Put the beets in a large saucepan and add enough cold salted water to cover them by 1 inch. Cover the saucepan and bring to a boil over high heat. Remove the lid and reduce the heat to medium-low. Simmer the beets, uncovered, until they are tender when pierced with the tip of a knife, about 45 minutes, depending on the size of the beets.

Drain the beets and let them cool until easy to handle. Slip the skins off the beets. Quarter the beets, and then cut them crosswise into 1- to 1½-inch chunks. (The beets can be covered and refrigerated for up to 2 days.)

Heat the oil in a large skillet over medium heat. Add the shallots and cook, stirring occasionally, until they are softened, about 2 minutes. Stir in the orange zest and juice, maple syrup, and vinegar. Add the beets and cook, stirring occasionally, until the liquid has reduced to a few tablespoons, about 10 minutes. Stir in the pecans and chives. Season to taste with salt and pepper. Transfer to a serving bowl, sprinkle with more pecans and chives, and serve.

Our family is split on broccoli. Some of us love it so much we eat it raw, straight from the fridge, stem and all. The rest of us generally avoid the verdant crucifer—except when it's prepared like this. The nutty, herby, garlicky combination is a wonderful way to show off broccoli's best side.

BROCCOLI with HAZELNUT TOPPING

MAKES 6 SERVINGS

1½ pounds broccoli crowns, cut into florets

3 tablespoons extra-virgin olive oil

2 tablespoons finely chopped shallots

1 garlic clove, minced

⅓ cup toasted, skinned, and coarsely chopped hazelnuts (see Note, page 132)

1 teaspoon pure maple syrup

1 teaspoon minced fresh thyme

¼ teaspoon red pepper flakes

¼ cup dry white wine

Fine sea salt

Bring a large pot of salted water to a boil over high heat. Add the broccoli and cook just until tender, about 5 minutes (or less, if you like the broccoli crisp). Drain, but do not rinse.

Meantime, heat 2 tablespoons of the oil in a medium skillet over medium heat. Add the shallots and the garlic and cook, stirring often, until the shallots are tender but not browned, 2 to 3 minutes. Add the hazelnuts, maple syrup, thyme, and red pepper flakes, and stir well. Add the wine and increase the heat to high. Boil, stirring often, until the wine has reduced to about 1 tablespoon, about 30 seconds. Season to taste with the salt. Remove from the heat.

Transfer the broccoli to a serving platter. Top the broccoli with the hazelnut mixture and drizzle with the remaining tablespoon oil. Serve immediately.

BROCCOLI is a member of the cruciferous vegetable family, and is among the most important anticancer foods. It has lots of vitamin A, C, and K and phytonutrients, which help reduce the risk of developing heart disease and diabetes. —MEHMET

Though my grandmother was Irish, she made some of the best Italian food I've ever eaten. Her most beloved dish was artichokes stuffed with garlic, bread crumbs, and oregano. She would use the same mouthwatering blend with clams or shrimp. Here I've paired that blend with cauliflower for a quick and easy taste of Italy. *Delizioso!!*

CAULIFLOWER OREGANATA

MAKES 6 SERVINGS

1 cauliflower (about 1½ pounds), cut into bite-size florets

Kosher salt

4 tablespoons extra-virgin olive oil

2 garlic cloves, finely chopped

2 teaspoons dried oregano

½ cup seasoned panko (Japanese bread crumbs)

¼ cup freshly grated Parmigiano-Reggiano cheese

1 tablespoon finely chopped fresh flat-leaf parsley

Finely grated zest of ½ lemon

½ teaspoon red pepper flakes

Position a rack in the center of the oven and preheat the oven to 350°F.

Bring a large saucepan of salted water to a boil over high heat. Add the cauliflower and cook until it is crisp-tender, 3 to 4 minutes. Drain the cauliflower, rinse under cold running water, and drain well. Pat the cauliflower dry with paper towels. Transfer the cauliflower to a shallow baking dish large enough to hold it in a single layer. Season the cauliflower to taste with the salt.

Heat 2 tablespoons of the oil in a medium skillet over medium-low heat. Add the garlic and cook, stirring often, until it is tender but not browned, about 1 minute. Stir in the oregano. Add the panko and mix well to coat with the seasoned oil. Remove from the heat and transfer to a bowl. Let the panko mixture cool slightly. Add the Parmigiano, parsley, lemon zest, and red pepper flakes, and mix well. Season to taste with salt.

Sprinkle the panko mixture evenly over the cauliflower and drizzle with the remaining 2 tablespoons oil. Bake until the crumbs are browned, about 25 minutes. Serve hot.

One of the problems with cooking Brussels sprouts is that the seasoning only reaches the outermost layer so the inner leaves remain quite bland. By chopping the sprouts, though, you ensure that the flavor is distributed throughout and every bite is delicious.

BRUSSELS SPROUTS CHIFFONADE with MAPLE SYRUP and THYME

MAKES 4 TO 6 SERVINGS

Two 10-ounce containers Brussels sprouts

1 tablespoon coconut oil

2 tablespoons finely chopped shallots

1½ teaspoons finely chopped fresh thyme

¼ teaspoon red pepper flakes

1 teaspoon pure maple syrup

Fine sea salt

Cut the Brussels sprouts crosswise into thin rounds. (Or use a food processor fitted with the slicing blade, and with the machine running, drop the Brussels sprouts through the feed tube to thinly slice them.)

Melt the oil in a large skillet over medium heat. Add the shallots and cook, stirring occasionally, until they are softened, about 2 minutes. Stir in the thyme and red pepper flakes. Add the Brussels sprouts, ½ cup water, and the maple syrup and mix well. Season to taste with the salt.

Cook, stirring occasionally, until the Brussels sprouts are tender and the water has evaporated, 12 to 15 minutes. Serve hot.

BRUSSELS SPROUTS This cruciferous vegetable is packed with flavonoids like lutein, zeaxanthin, and indoles, which help protect against certain cancers. They are extremely low in calories yet provide an abundant source of vitamins, minerals, and fiber. —MEHMET

I love this simple Thai-inspired dish with its honeyed carrots, pungent ginger, and tart squirt of fresh lime. Please make sure to use unsweetened coconut, as the regular supermarket flakes are too sugary. Of course, standard carrots cut into 1½-inch lengths can stand in for the baby carrots; and if you are not a cilantro fan, try these with mint or Thai basil instead.

BABY CARROTS with COCONUT and GINGER

MAKES 4 TO 6 SERVINGS

3 tablespoons desiccated coconut or unsweetened coconut shreds

1 pound baby carrots

1 tablespoon honey

1 tablespoon fresh lime juice

2 scallions (white and green parts), finely chopped

1 tablespoon finely chopped fresh cilantro

2 teaspoons peeled and minced fresh ginger

Fine sea salt and freshly ground black pepper

Heat a medium skillet over medium heat. Add the coconut and cook, stirring almost constantly, until it is toasted, about 2 minutes. Transfer the coconut to a plate and set aside.

Half-fill the skillet with salted water and bring it to a boil over high heat. Add the carrots and cover the skillet. Cook until the carrots are barely tender, 5 to 7 minutes. Drain the carrots in a colander and return them to the skillet.

Drizzle the honey and lime juice over the carrots and mix well. Add the scallions, cilantro, and ginger and mix again. Season to taste with salt and pepper. Transfer the carrots to a serving bowl, and sprinkle with the toasted coconut. Serve hot.

HONEY is antibacterial, antifungal, and antiviral. Some studies have shown it to be as effective as cough syrup, and it may help with gastrointestinal disorders as well. Make sure to look for unpasteurized versions, as heating the honey denatures the protective proteins and enzymes.
—MEHMET

Here, cauliflower is dressed up with the sultry flavors of a Middle Eastern spice market. We like to cook it to a deep golden brown so the tips get nice and crispy.

ROASTED SWEET and SAVORY CAULIFLOWER

MAKES 6 SERVINGS

¼ cup coconut oil

4 shallots, thinly sliced (1 cup)

4 garlic cloves, minced

1 tablespoon ground cumin

1 tablespoon honey

1 tablespoon fresh lemon juice

¼ teaspoon red pepper flakes

1 cauliflower (about 1½ pounds), cut into bite-size florets

Fine sea salt and freshly ground black pepper

½ cup pine nuts

½ cup dried currants or golden raisins

Position a rack in the center of the oven and preheat to 400°F.

Melt the oil in a large skillet over medium heat. Add the shallots and cook, stirring occasionally, until they are softened, about 2 minutes. Stir in the garlic and cook until it is fragrant, about 1 minute. Add the cumin and mix until it gives off its aroma, about 30 seconds. Stir in the honey, lemon juice, and red pepper flakes.

Put the cauliflower in a 9 by 13-inch baking dish. Pour the cumin mixture over the cauliflower, season to taste with salt and black pepper, and mix well. Spread the cauliflower mixture in the dish.

Bake, stirring occasionally, until the cauliflower is a golden brown and just tender, about 30 minutes. During the last 5 minutes or so of baking, stir in the pine nuts and currants. Serve hot.

CAULIFLOWER reduces inflammation and helps the body detox. Its glucosinolates support liver function, while its high fiber content aids in elimination, flushing toxins out of the body. —MEHMET

This is a light, citrus-splashed update of the classic green beans almondine. I prefer the haricots verts because they have a crisp, firm texture and a subtler flavor than the standard variety of green bean.

HARICOTS VERTS with ORANGE, ALMONDS, and CORIANDER

MAKES 6 SERVINGS

12 ounces haricots verts, stems trimmed

1 tablespoon extra-virgin olive oil

3 tablespoons finely chopped shallots

2 garlic cloves, finely chopped

¼ cup sliced natural almonds

Grated zest of ½ orange

2 tablespoons fresh orange juice

½ teaspoon ground coriander

⅛ teaspoon red pepper flakes

Fine sea salt

Bring a large saucepan of salted water to a boil over high heat. Add the haricots verts and cook just until they turn bright green and are crisp-tender, about 2 minutes. Drain and rinse under cold running water. Drain again and pat them dry with paper towels.

Heat the oil in a large skillet over medium heat. Add the shallots and garlic and cook, stirring occasionally, until the shallots are tender, about 2 minutes. Stir in the almonds, orange zest and juice, coriander, and red pepper flakes. Add the green beans and cook, stirring occasionally, until they are reheated, about 3 minutes. Season to taste with salt and serve.

Redolent with cumin and oregano, these spiced veggies are a favorite at family gatherings during the holidays. They go fast, so I always make a big batch. I like this combination of butternut squash, sweet potatoes, and carrots, but you can use less-sweet root vegetables, like turnips, parsnips, and golden beets, if you prefer.

ROASTED SAVORY VEGETABLES

MAKES 6 TO 8 SERVINGS

1 small butternut squash (about 2 pounds), peeled, seeded, and cut into 1-inch pieces

1 pound orange-fleshed sweet potatoes, peeled and cut into 1-inch chunks

1 pound fingerling or other small potatoes, halved

5 medium carrots, cut into 1-inch lengths

4 large shallots, peeled and halved lengthwise

¼ cup extra-virgin olive oil

12 garlic cloves, coarsely chopped

2 teaspoons dried oregano

1 teaspoon balsamic vinegar

1 teaspoon nigella seeds

1 teaspoon cumin seeds

½ teaspoon ground cumin

¼ teaspoon red pepper flakes

Fine sea salt

Position a rack in the center of the oven and preheat the oven to 425°F.

Combine the squash, sweet potatoes, fingerling potatoes, carrots, and shallots in a 15 by 10 by 2-inch glass or ceramic baking dish. Whisk the oil, garlic, oregano, vinegar, nigella seeds, cumin seeds, ground cumin, and red pepper flakes together in a small bowl. Pour over the vegetables and mix well. Season with ½ teaspoon salt. The vegetables will be crowded in the dish.

Bake, stirring occasionally, until the vegetables are tender when pierced with the tip of a knife, about 45 minutes. Season to taste with salt and serve hot.

Candied sweet potatoes were always a standard at holiday gatherings, but over time our taste buds grew up and we wanted something a little more sophisticated. This version has a fragrant blend of spices with just a hint of honey. The crunch of pomegranate seeds gives interest to the otherwise smooth-textured dish.

SPICED MASHED SWEET POTATOES with POMEGRANATE

MAKES 4 TO 6 SERVINGS

4 medium orange-fleshed sweet potatoes (about 2½ pounds)

1 tablespoon coconut oil, melted

1 teaspoon honey

½ teaspoon pomegranate molasses

½ teaspoon ground cinnamon

⅛ teaspoon ground cardamom

Fine sea salt

½ cup pomegranate arils (seeds), from ½ pomegranate (see Note, page 104)

Position a rack in the center of the oven and preheat the oven to 400°F.

Pierce each sweet potato a few times with a fork. Place them on a rimmed baking sheet. Bake until the potatoes are tender when pierced with the tip of a small sharp knife, about 45 minutes.

Peel the sweet potatoes and transfer the flesh to a medium bowl. Mash the sweet potatoes with a potato masher or a large fork. Mix in the coconut oil, honey, pomegranate molasses, cinnamon, and cardamom. Season lightly to taste with the salt. Transfer to a serving bowl, top with the pomegranate seeds, and serve.

SWEET POTATOES are rich in beta-carotene, vitamin A, and vitamin C to keep your immune system strong.
—MEHMET

These have the look and feel of French fries but are so much more flavorful. The fact that they're more healthful, too, is almost irrelevant. Be sure to spread the sweet potatoes out between two baking sheets—if they are crowded, they will steam and not brown.

SPICED SWEET POTATO OVEN FRIES
with GARLICKY YOGURT DIP

MAKES 4 TO 6 SERVINGS

GARLICKY YOGURT DIP

One 7-ounce container plain Greek yogurt (¾ cup plus 2 tablespoons)

1 teaspoon tahini

½ teaspoon honey

1 garlic clove, crushed through a garlic press

Kosher salt, to taste

3 large orange-fleshed sweet potatoes

1 tablespoon extra-virgin olive oil, plus more for the baking sheets

2 teaspoons dried oregano

½ teaspoon red pepper flakes

Kosher salt

Position racks in the top third and center of the oven and preheat the oven to 400°F.

To make the dip: Mix the yogurt, tahini, honey, and garlic together in a small bowl. Season to taste with salt. Let stand at room temperature to blend the flavors while preparing the sweet potatoes.

Peel the sweet potatoes. Trim off and discard the pointed tips (they tend to burn during roasting). Using a large knife, cut each sweet potato lengthwise into slabs about ½ inch thick, and then into fries about ½ inch wide. Lightly oil two large rimmed baking sheets.

Toss the potatoes with the oil in a large bowl. Add the oregano and red pepper flakes, and toss again, seasoning the fries with 1 teaspoon salt. Divide the sweet potatoes between the baking sheets, spreading them out in single layers. Bake, flipping the fries over halfway through cooking, until they are tender and browned, about 40 minutes.

Serve the sweet potatoes immediately with the dip.

YOGURT *feeds your gut. We have ten times more bacteria in our gut than cells in our body, and so we effectively outsource our digestion to these visitors. Most of them desire to help us, but we have at least 500 species that are lethal. The bad guys are kept at bay by the much more numerous good guys, but you have to feed the defending armies with probiotics, which occur naturally in yogurt, kefir, sauerkraut, pickles, and fermented tofu.* —**MEHMET**

PASTAS AND GRAINS

Farro is an Italian grain similar to spelt, and it has the same chewy texture and nutty flavor. It partners beautifully with woodsy sautéed mushrooms like shiitake, cremini, or portobellos (which are just larger, older cremini).

FARRO with MUSHROOMS and THYME

MAKES 4 TO 6 SERVINGS

2 tablespoons extra-virgin olive oil

1 pound shiitake or cremini mushrooms, sliced

1/3 cup finely chopped shallots or yellow onion

1 tablespoon finely chopped fresh thyme, plus sprigs for garnish

1 garlic clove, minced

4 1/2 cups Basic Farro (page 274)

Fine sea salt and freshly ground black pepper

Heat the oil in a large skillet over medium heat. Add the mushrooms and cook, stirring occasionally, until they give off their liquid and begin to brown, about 8 minutes. Stir in the shallots, chopped thyme, and garlic and cook until the shallots are tender, about 2 minutes.

Add the farro and cook, stirring occasionally, until the farro is heated through, about 5 minutes if the farro is chilled, or less if it is hot and freshly cooked. Season to taste with salt and pepper. Serve hot, garnishing each serving with a thyme sprig.

SHIITAKE MUSHROOMS are great immune boosters, and some studies have shown that they may be helpful in reducing cancer. Mushrooms are also a good food source of vitamin D, which we can usually get only from the sun.
—MEHMET

When Arabella was living in London, she fell in love with the food of Yotam Ottolenghi, whose eponymous restaurant was just down the block from her flat. This fragrant pasta recipe is inspired by his Tagliatelle with Spiced Butter. Our version leaves out the butter, but includes soft cubes of butternut squash.

CURRIED FETTUCCINE with ROASTED SQUASH, CHICKPEAS, and HAZELNUTS

MAKES 4 SERVINGS

½ large butternut squash, top part only (save the bulbous end for another use), peeled and cut into 1-inch cubes (about 4 cups)

¼ cup plus 1 tablespoon extra-virgin olive oil

½ cup finely chopped shallots

2 garlic cloves, thinly sliced

1½ teaspoons ground cumin

1½ teaspoons ground coriander

1 teaspoon ground ginger or ½ teaspoon grated fresh

½ teaspoon ground turmeric

⅛ teaspoon ground cinnamon

¼ teaspoon red pepper flakes

One 15-ounce can chickpeas (garbanzo beans), drained and rinsed

½ cup dry white wine

½ cup toasted, skinned, and chopped hazelnuts (see Note, page 132)

3 tablespoons finely chopped fresh mint, plus more for garnish

3 tablespoons finely chopped fresh chives, plus more for garnish

1 pound standard or gluten-free dried fettuccine

Fine sea salt and freshly ground black pepper

Position a rack in the center of the oven and preheat the oven to 400°F.

Toss the squash and 1 tablespoon of the oil in a large bowl. Spread the squash in a 10 by 15-inch baking dish. Bake, stirring occasionally, until the squash is tender, but not particularly browned, about 45 minutes.

Bring a large pot of salted water to a boil over high heat.

(recipe continues)

Meanwhile, heat the remaining ¼ cup oil in a large skillet over medium-low heat. Add the shallots and garlic and cook, stirring occasionally, until they are softened but not browned, about 2 minutes. Add the cumin, coriander, ginger, turmeric, cinnamon, and red pepper flakes and stir well. Stir in the chickpeas, wine, and hazelnuts, and bring to a simmer. Stir in the mint and chives. Remove from the heat and cover with the lid ajar to keep the sauce warm.

Add the fettuccine to the pot of boiling water and cook according to the package directions, stirring occasionally, until al dente. Drain the pasta and add it to the skillet with the sauce. Toss well, and season to taste with salt and pepper. Serve the pasta hot in individual bowls, sprinkling each serving with additional mint and chives.

BLACK PEPPER aids in digestion, reducing the production of gas and encouraging the removal of toxins through perspiration and urination. It can also help fight off a cold and speed up your metabolism. —**MEHMET**

Mehmet jokingly calls me a "carbotarian" because, given my choice, I'd eat pasta every day. (I don't do it . . . but I would.) This is hands-down my favorite sauce because it is both incredibly easy and utterly delicious. The key is using fresh, vine-ripened tomatoes. Pick some up at your local farmers' market or produce store. And remember to include plenty of basil!

PENNE with QUICK TOMATO and BASIL SAUCE

MAKES 4 TO 6 SERVINGS

TOMATO AND BASIL SAUCE

2 tablespoons extra-virgin olive oil

1 medium yellow onion, finely chopped

2 garlic cloves, thinly sliced

2 pounds ripe tomatoes

Kosher salt and freshly ground black pepper

1/3 cup finely chopped fresh basil

1 pound dried penne (or pasta of your choice)

Freshly grated Parmigiano-Reggiano, for serving

Bring a large pot of lightly salted water to a boil over high heat.

Meanwhile, make the sauce: Heat the oil in a wide, deep skillet over medium heat. Add the onion and cook, stirring occasionally, until it has softened, about 3 minutes. Stir in the garlic and cook until it is fragrant, about 1 minute.

While the onion mixture is cooking, core the tomatoes and cut them into ¾-inch dice, saving the juices. When the garlic is fragrant, add the diced tomatoes and their juices, season to taste with salt and pepper, and bring the mixture to a boil over high heat. Reduce the heat to medium and cook at a brisk simmer, stirring occasionally, until the tomato juices have thickened, 10 to 15 minutes.

Add the penne to the boiling water and cook according to the package directions until the pasta is al dente. Drain well.

Stir the basil into the sauce. Transfer the penne to a large serving bowl. Add the sauce and mix well. Serve immediately with the Parmigiano passed on the side.

These fabulous little dumplings are ideal for a holiday feast or other special occasion. Making the gnocchi from scratch is a bit more work than using a packaged type, but the delicately spiced flavor of the butternut squash is hard to replicate in a store-bought version.

GNOCCHI with WALNUT and SAGE SAUCE

MAKES 6 TO 8 SERVINGS

GNOCCHI

1 medium butternut squash (about 2 pounds), peeled, seeded, and cut into 2-inch chunks

1 tablespoon extra-virgin olive oil

1 large egg and 1 large egg yolk

¾ teaspoon fine sea salt

Pinch of ground cinnamon

Pinch of ground cloves

Pinch of ground cardamom (optional)

1¼ cups unbleached all-purpose flour, as needed, plus more for shaping the gnocchi

SAUCE

2 tablespoons extra-virgin olive oil

12 large fresh sage leaves

2 tablespoons unsalted butter

2 tablespoons finely chopped shallots

½ cup toasted and chopped walnuts (see Note, page 162)

1 teaspoon pure maple syrup

Fine sea salt and freshly ground black pepper

Freshly grated Parmigiano-Reggiano, for serving

Position a rack in the center of the oven and preheat the oven to 400°F.

To make the gnocchi: Toss the squash with the oil on a large rimmed baking sheet to coat well. Bake, stirring occasionally, until the squash is tender but not deeply browned, about 30 minutes. Let the squash cool. Purée the cooled squash in a food processor. Measure 1½ cups squash; reserve the remaining squash for another use.

Whisk the squash purée, egg and egg yolk, salt, cinnamon, cloves, and cardamom, if using, together in a large bowl. Gradually stir in enough of the flour to make a soft dough that holds its shape when rolled into a rope. Do not add too much flour or the gnocchi will be tough.

Dust the work surface and a large rimmed baking sheet with flour. Divide the dough into sixths. Working with

(recipe continues)

NOTE To toast the walnuts, spread them on a rimmed baking sheet. Bake in a preheated 350°F oven, stirring them occasionally, until they are toasted and fragrant, 12 to 15 minutes.

one portion at a time, place the dough on the work surface. Roll the dough underneath your palms into a rope about ½ inch thick. Cut the rope into 1-inch lengths. Transfer the gnocchi to the baking sheet, being sure they are not touching. (If you wish, pick up the gnocchi, one at a time, and press the tines of a fork into each to make ridges.) Cover the gnocchi loosely with plastic wrap and refrigerate until ready to cook (up to 6 hours).

Bring a large pot of salted water to a boil over high heat.

Meanwhile, make the sauce: Heat the oil in a large skillet over medium-high heat until the oil is shimmering but not smoking. Add the sage and cook until the leaves are crisp, about 15 seconds. Using a slotted spoon, transfer the sage leaves to paper towels to drain.

Reduce the heat to medium. Add the butter to the sage-flavored oil. Add the shallots and cook until tender and lightly browned, about 2 minutes. Add the walnuts and maple syrup and stir well. Season to taste with salt and pepper. Remove the skillet from the heat and cover with the lid ajar.

A handful at a time, add the gnocchi to the boiling water. Cook until the gnocchi have all floated to the top of the water. Continue cooking from this point until the gnocchi are tender and cooked through, about 2 minutes. Scoop out and reserve ½ cup of the cooking water. Drain the gnocchi well, but do not rinse them.

Transfer the gnocchi to the skillet. Heat over medium heat, stirring gently to avoid breaking the gnocchi. Add enough of the reserved cooking water to thin the sauce, and stir until the gnocchi are lightly coated. Divide among serving bowls. Crush the fried sage leaves and sprinkle them over each serving. Serve with the Parmigiano on the side.

This dish is elegant and sophisticated, and perfect for company when you want to impress. It takes a bit of effort to stuff all the squares, so enlist extra hands to help. (Good luck if one of those helpers is a fifteen-year-old boy.)

EDAMAME WONTONS with TRUFFLE and WINE SAUCE

MAKES 8 TO 10 SERVINGS

WONTONS

1 pound frozen shelled edamame

1 tablespoon unsalted butter

3 tablespoons finely chopped shallots

¼ cup plain Greek yogurt

2 tablespoons truffle-flavored oil

2 tablespoons finely chopped chives

Kosher salt and freshly ground black pepper

Cornstarch, for dusting

About 60 square wonton wrappers

TRUFFLE AND WINE SAUCE

3 tablespoons unsalted butter

3 tablespoons minced shallots

2 teaspoons finely chopped fresh thyme

¼ cup dry white wine

3 tablespoons extra-virgin olive oil

2 tablespoons truffle-flavored oil

2 tablespoons finely chopped fresh chives

Kosher salt and freshly ground black pepper

Freshly grated Parmigiano-Reggiano cheese, for serving

To make the wontons: Bring a large saucepan of salted water to a boil over high heat. Add the edamame and cook according to the package directions until they are tender, about 10 minutes. Scoop out and reserve about ½ cup of the cooking liquid. Drain the edamame, rinse under cold running water, and drain again. Pat the edamame dry with paper towels.

Melt the butter in a medium skillet over medium-low heat. Add the shallots and cook, stirring occasionally, until they are tender but not browned, about 3 minutes. Add the edamame and shallots to a food processor and pulse until the edamame are finely chopped. Add the yogurt and truffle oil and process, adding a few tablespoons of the reserved cooking water, as needed, to make a smooth, thick paste. Add the chives and pulse

(recipe continues)

just until combined. Season to taste with salt and pepper. Transfer the filling to a medium bowl.

Line a baking sheet with parchment or wax paper and dust the paper with cornstarch. Fill a ramekin with water.

For each wonton, place a wonton square on the work surface, with two points facing north and south. Spoon a teaspoon of the filling in the middle of the square. Lightly brush the edges of the square with water and bring the north and south points together to enclose the filling. Bring up the east and west points, and close all the sides. Transfer the wonton to the baking sheet. Do not let the wontons touch each other. Loosely cover the wontons with plastic wrap and refrigerate until ready to cook, up to 4 hours.

To make the sauce: Melt the butter in a large skillet over medium-low heat. Add the shallots and cook, stirring occasionally, until tender but not browned, about 3 minutes. Stir in the thyme. Add the wine and bring it to a boil. Stir in ½ cup water and the olive oil, and bring to a boil over high heat. Remove from the heat and cover to keep warm.

Meanwhile, bring a large pot of salted water to a boil. Taking care that the wontons do not stick together, add them to the boiling water and return the water to a boil. When all of the wontons are floating in the water, cook them until tender, about 1 minute. Carefully drain the water; do not rinse the wontons under cold water.

Transfer the drained wontons to the skillet. Drizzle them with the truffle oil and sprinkle in the chives. Mix gently, just to coat the wontons with the sauce, seasoning to taste with salt and pepper.

Serve hot with the cheese on the side.

One of the things I love about this bowl is that it is totally flexible. Use the veggies I've suggested here or substitute with whatever you've got in the fridge. Other great options include bell peppers, green beans, cabbage, scallions, and snow peas. They all benefit from a toss with ginger and garlic. A drizzle of tahini sauce makes them downright delectable.

BROWN RICE with VEGETABLE STIR-FRY and TAHINI-MISO SAUCE

MAKES 4 SERVINGS

TAHINI-MISO SAUCE

3 tablespoons tahini

3 tablespoons white (shiro) miso

2 tablespoons fresh lemon juice

2 teaspoons tamari or soy sauce

1 teaspoon fresh ginger juice (see Note, page 125)

2 garlic cloves, minced

Fine sea salt

STIR-FRY

1 pound broccoli crowns, cut into bite-size florets

2 tablespoons extra-virgin olive oil

1 teaspoon peeled and minced fresh ginger

2 garlic cloves, minced

8 ounces shiitake mushrooms, stems discarded, caps cut into 1/4-inch slices

1 medium yellow onion, cut into thin half-moons

1 Shanghai (baby) bok choy, cut crosswise into 1/2-inch slices

1/2 cup coarsely chopped raw cashews

2 tablespoons tamari or soy sauce

1 teaspoon pure maple syrup

1/4 teaspoon red pepper flakes

Fine sea salt

4 to 6 cups hot Basic Brown Rice (page 275)

Finely chopped fresh cilantro, for garnish

To make the sauce: Whisk the tahini, miso, lemon juice, tamari, ginger juice, and garlic together with 1/4 cup water in a small bowl. Season to taste with salt. Set aside.

To make the stir-fry: Bring a medium saucepan of salted water to a boil over high heat.

Add the broccoli and boil just until it is crisp-tender and bright green, about 3 minutes. Drain in a colander, rinse under cold water, and drain again.

Heat the oil in a large skillet over high heat until the oil is very hot but not smoking. Add the ginger and garlic and stir until they are fragrant, about 15 seconds. Add the mushrooms and onion and cook, stirring often, until the onion softens, about 3 minutes. Add the bok choy and cook until it is beginning to wilt, about 1 minute. Stir in the reserved broccoli along with the cashews and cook for another minute. Add the tamari, maple syrup, and red pepper flakes. Season to taste with the salt. Remove from the heat.

Divide the rice among four bowls. Top each with the stir-fry, and sprinkle with the cilantro. Serve with the sauce on the side for drizzling.

CILANTRO *is a natural detoxifier, which can help rid the body of heavy metals like lead. It is also a potent source of vitamin K, an essential nutrient for bone strength and cardiovascular health.* **—MEHMET**

This typical mingling of cool, creamy coconut milk with fiery red curry paste transforms plain rice and vegetables into something truly magical.

BROWN RICE BOWL with RED CURRY VEGETABLES

MAKES 4 SERVINGS

VEGETABLE CURRY

3 medium carrots, cut into ¼-inch rounds

2 tablespoons coconut oil

½ cup finely chopped shallots

3 scallions (white and green parts), finely chopped

2 garlic cloves, minced

2 teaspoons peeled and finely shredded fresh ginger (use the small holes on a box grater)

½ large red bell pepper, cut into ½-inch dice

6 button mushrooms, cut into quarters

1 Shanghai (baby) bok choy, cut crosswise into ½-inch slices

1 tablespoon red curry paste

One 14-ounce can light coconut milk

Fine sea salt

4 to 6 cups hot Basic Brown Rice (page 275)

2 tablespoons chopped fresh cilantro

To make the vegetable curry: Bring a medium saucepan of salted water to a boil over high heat. Add the carrots and cook for about 2 minutes. Drain in a colander and rinse under cold running water.

Heat the oil in a large skillet or wok over medium heat. Add the shallots, scallions, garlic, and ginger and cook, stirring often, until the shallots soften, about 1 minute. Add the reserved carrots along with the red pepper and mushrooms and cook, stirring occasionally, until the pepper softens, about 2 minutes. Add the bok choy and cook, stirring often, until it is crisp-tender, about 2 minutes.

Move the vegetable mixture to one side of the skillet. Drop the curry paste on the empty side of the skillet and stir until it sizzles, about 15 seconds. Pour the coconut milk over the curry paste and stir to dissolve the paste. Mix the coconut mixture with the vegetables and bring to a boil. Season to taste with the salt. Remove from the heat and partially cover to keep warm.

Divide the rice among four bowls and top with the curry. Sprinkle with the cilantro and serve.

The first time I ordered *pasta alla puttanesca* was simply because of its name. As an adolescent girl, I found something intriguing about eating the meal of a "street-walker." It felt daring and provocative. Wonderfully, it tasted that way, too, with its sour and salty blend of capers, olives, and anchovies. I missed it terribly once I stopped eating fish—until I discovered I could substitute seaweed for the anchovies and still get that tangy oceanic flavor.

SPAGHETTI with VEGETARIAN PUTTANESCA SAUCE

MAKES 4 TO 6 SERVINGS

PUTTANESCA SAUCE

1 tablespoon extra-virgin olive oil

1 medium yellow onion, finely chopped

3 garlic cloves, thinly sliced

1 teaspoon dried oregano

¼ teaspoon red pepper flakes, or more to taste

One 28-ounce can crushed tomatoes

2 teaspoons finely crushed roasted seaweed salad sprinkles

½ cup pitted and coarsely chopped olives, preferably Kalamata

2 tablespoons rinsed and drained nonpareil capers

1 pound dried spaghetti or linguine

1 teaspoon balsamic vinegar

To make the sauce: Heat the oil in a large skillet over medium heat. Add the onion and cook, stirring occasionally, until it has softened, about 3 minutes. Stir in the garlic, oregano, and red pepper flakes and cook until the garlic is fragrant, about 1 minute. Stir in the tomatoes and seaweed and bring to a simmer. Lower the heat to medium-low and simmer, stirring occasionally, until the sauce has slightly reduced, about 20 minutes. During the last 5 minutes, stir in the olives and capers.

Meanwhile, bring a large pot of salted water to a boil over high heat. Add the spaghetti and cook according to the package directions until the pasta is al dente. Drain well.

Stir the vinegar into the sauce. Transfer the spaghetti to a large serving bowl. Add the sauce and mix well. Serve immediately.

RED PEPPER FLAKES *Beat the sugar cravings by incorporating mood-boosting red pepper flakes into your diet. The capsaicin in chili peppers will give you a feel-good rush that's similar to the dopamine boost you get from eating a cookie.* —MEHMET

Millet is a marvelous grain. It has a texture similar to couscous, but it is gluten free and high in protein, minerals, and fiber. Its mellow taste is a great base for a variety of seasonings and flavors. In this recipe I mix millet with basil, garlic, and pine nuts for a light, fresh alternative to pasta with pesto.

MILLET with DECONSTRUCTED PESTO

MAKES 4 TO 6 SERVINGS

1 cup millet

Fine sea salt

¼ cup pine nuts, toasted (see Note, page 130)

⅓ cup finely chopped fresh basil

3 tablespoons extra-virgin olive oil

3 tablespoons freshly grated pecorino romano cheese

1 garlic clove, minced

Bring the millet, 2 cups water, and ½ teaspoon salt to a boil in a medium saucepan over high heat. Reduce the heat to low and cover. Simmer until the millet is tender and has absorbed the liquid, about 20 minutes. Remove from the heat and let stand for 5 minutes. Fluff the millet with a fork.

Add the pine nuts, basil, oil, cheese, and garlic to the millet and mix well. Transfer the mixture to a serving bowl and serve.

PINE NUTS contain pinolenic acid, a fat that stimulates the hormone cholecystokinin (CCK), which suppresses appetite. They are also loaded with protein, magnesium, and antioxidants. —MEHMET

Quinoa seems to be the queen of grains right now. (Sort of the way kale is the king of greens.) And the position is not undeserved. It's versatile, nutrient dense, and most important, delicious! Here, quinoa is highlighted with a sprinkling of tart cherries and crunchy pecans. (Note: this is another fabulous bowl for layering protein "add-ins.")

WARM QUINOA and CHICKPEAS

MAKES 6 TO 8 SERVINGS

1 1/2 cups quinoa, preferably rainbow

2 tablespoons coconut oil

1/4 cup finely chopped shallots

Fine sea salt

One 15-ounce can chickpeas (garbanzo beans), drained and rinsed

3 scallions (white and green parts), finely chopped

1/2 cup coarsely chopped pecans

1/2 cup coarsely chopped dried tart cherries

2 tablespoons fresh orange juice

Freshly ground black pepper

Place the quinoa in a fine-mesh sieve and rinse it well under cold running water. Drain well and set aside.

Melt the oil in a medium saucepan over medium heat. Add the shallots and cook, stirring often until they are tender, about 3 minutes. Add the rinsed quinoa, 3 cups water, and 3/4 teaspoon salt. Bring to a boil over high heat. Reduce the heat to low and cover the saucepan. Simmer, without stirring, until the liquid is absorbed and the quinoa is tender, about 25 minutes. Remove the saucepan from the heat. Add the chickpeas, scallions, pecans, cherries, and orange juice, but do not stir them in. Let stand for 5 minutes.

Fluff the quinoa with a fork, mixing in the added ingredients, and season with salt and pepper. Serve warm.

PECANS Pecans are high in omega-3s and are the most antioxidant-rich tree nut. They have been shown to reduce the risk of neural degeneration and may help prevent brain-related diseases such as stroke, depression, and anxiety. —**MEHMET**

This pungent, aromatic dish has an almost porridge-like texture that makes it extremely satisfying. It's our version of Indian comfort food!

QUINOA with MUNG BEANS and INDIAN SPICES

MAKES 4 SERVINGS

½ cup quinoa

1 tablespoon coconut oil

1 small yellow onion, finely chopped

2 garlic cloves, minced

1 teaspoon ground coriander

½ teaspoon ground cumin

½ teaspooon ground turmeric

¼ teaspoon ground ginger

½ teaspoon fine sea salt

½ cup split dried mung beans

Chopped fresh cilantro, for serving

Place the quinoa in a fine-mesh wire sieve and rinse it well under cold running water. Drain well and set aside.

Melt the oil in a medium saucepan over medium heat. Add the onion and garlic and cook, stirring occasionally, until the onion is translucent, about 4 minutes. Add the coriander, cumin, turmeric, ginger, and salt and stir until the spices give off their fragrance, about 15 seconds.

Add the rinsed quinoa and the mung beans and stir well. Add 2½ cups water and bring to a boil over high heat. Reduce the heat to low and cover the saucepan. Simmer, without stirring, until the liquid is absorbed and the mung beans are barely tender, about 25 minutes. Transfer to a serving bowl, top with the cilantro, and serve hot.

QUINOA is popular throughout South America, and is packed with protein and fiber. It's also a rich source of minerals like manganese, magnesium, and phosphorus, as well as flavonoids including quercetin. Quinoa is naturally gluten free, so it makes a great wheat substitute.
—MEHMET

This is my take on the Spanish classic, paella. While I've kept the customary saffron threads, I've added the duskier notes of cumin and some citrus-scented coriander. I also use brown rice (which would appall the traditionalists). This version calls for shrimp, but you know you can replace it with your protein of choice.

FRIED RICE PAELLA with SPICED CHICKPEAS and SHRIMP

MAKES 4 SERVINGS

1 tablespoon tomato paste

1/2 teaspoon coarsely crushed saffron threads

1/2 cup dry white wine

2 tablespoons extra-virgin olive oil

1 medium yellow onion, finely chopped

2 medium carrots, cut into 1/8-inch dice

2 scallions (white and green parts), thinly sliced

3 garlic cloves, minced

1/2 teaspoon ground cumin

1/2 teaspoon ground coriander

1/8 teaspoon cayenne pepper

4 cups chilled Basic Brown Rice (page 275; see Note)

1 pound cooked shrimp, preferably Quick Shrimp with Garlic and Lemon (page 271)

Spiced Baked Chickpeas (page 273)

3 tablespoons finely chopped fresh cilantro, plus more for garnish

Fine sea salt and freshly ground black pepper

Whisk 1/4 cup warm water, the tomato paste, and saffron together in a small bowl to dissolve the tomato paste. Add the wine and set the bowl aside.

Heat the oil in a large nonstick skillet over medium heat. Add the onion and carrots and cover. Cook, stirring occasionally, until the carrots soften, about 4 minutes. Stir in the scallions and garlic and cook, uncovered, until the garlic is fragrant, about 1 minute.

Stir in the cumin, coriander, and cayenne and cook until they give off their aroma, about 15 seconds. Add the brown rice and mix well. Drizzle in the wine mixture and cook, stirring often, until the rice is hot, 3 to 4 minutes. Add the shrimp and chickpeas and cook until they are just heated through, about 1 minute more. Stir in the cilantro. Season to taste with salt and pepper. Spoon into bowls and serve, sprinkling each with more cilantro.

NOTE The rice must be cold or at cool room temperature, or it will clump together when stir-fried. If you are using frozen rice, on the morning of cooking, let the rice thaw in the refrigerator all day so it is ready in the evening when you want to cook it for dinner. Or, thaw the rice just before cooking in a microwave oven: Transfer the rice to a microwave-safe bowl. Heat at medium (50 percent) power, occasionally separating any clumps with your fingers, until the rice is cool, but not hot, about 5 minutes.

MAIN COURSES

I love this vegan casserole, with its comforting mix of black beans and mushrooms under a soft cap of cornbread. You can also substitute different kinds of beans—say, kidney, pinto, or navy. Remember that the filling's liquid will evaporate a bit during baking, so check it and stop the cooking before it gets dry. It should be on the juicy side.

BLACK BEAN CASSEROLE
with CILANTRO-CORNBREAD TOPPING

MAKES 6 SERVINGS

FILLING

2 tablespoons extra-virgin olive oil, plus more for the baking dish

10 ounces cremini mushrooms, quartered

1 large yellow onion, finely chopped

1 medium red bell pepper, cut into ½-inch dice

3 garlic cloves, minced

2 teaspoons ground cumin

2 teaspoons ground coriander

2 teaspoons dried oregano

Three 15-ounce cans black beans, drained and rinsed

2 cups All-Purpose Vegetable Broth (page 278) or water

Fine sea salt and freshly ground black pepper

CORNBREAD TOPPING

⅓ cup plus 1 tablespoon boiling water

2 tablespoons ground flaxseeds

1¼ cups canned coconut milk

2 tablespoons pure maple syrup

1 cup yellow cornmeal

1 cup unbleached all-purpose flour

4 teaspoons baking powder

1 teaspoon chili powder

½ teaspoon fine sea salt

2 tablespoons finely chopped fresh cilantro, plus more for serving

To make the filling: Heat the oil in a large skillet over medium-high heat. Add the mushrooms and cook, stirring occasionally, until they begin to brown, about 8 minutes. Stir in the onion, bell pepper, and garlic and cook, stirring occasionally, until the onion softens, about 3 minutes more. Stir in the cumin, coriander, and oregano.

Add the beans and broth and bring to a boil. Reduce the heat to medium-low and simmer, stirring occasionally, to blend the flavors without substantially evaporating the liquid, about 10 minutes. Season to taste with salt and pepper. Lightly oil a 9 by 13-inch baking dish. Transfer the filling to the prepared dish.

Position a rack in the top third of the oven and preheat the oven to 350°F.

Meanwhile, make the topping: Whisk the boiling water and ground flaxseeds together in a small bowl and set aside to thicken for about 5 minutes. Transfer the mixture to a medium bowl, add the coconut milk and maple syrup, and whisk well.

Whisk together the cornmeal, flour, baking powder, chili powder, and salt in a second medium bowl. Add the coconut milk mixture and stir with a wooden spoon just until combined. Fold in the cilantro. Drop six large, wide dollops of the batter, spaced equally apart (the batter will spread during baking), over the top of the filling.

Bake until the cornbread topping is golden brown and a wooden toothpick inserted in the center comes out clean, 35 to 40 minutes. Let stand for 5 minutes. Spoon the filling, with the cornbread topping, into bowls, sprinkle with the cilantro, and serve.

BLACK BEANS High in flavonoids, protein, and fiber, black beans are great for the digestive tract and regulation of blood sugar. They're also packed with anthocyanins, which might help ward off chronic illnesses like Parkinson's disease. —MEHMET

This brilliant green chimichurri sauce is delicious on just about anything. I've served it with fish, meat, chicken, and beans. Here, it's paired with a crispy-coated tofu for a mouthwatering vegetarian entrée.

ALMOND-CRUSTED TOFU
with CILANTRO CHIMICHURRI

MAKES 4 SERVINGS

CHIMICHURRI

2 cups packed fresh cilantro leaves

2 tablespoons fresh lime juice

2 garlic cloves, minced

2 teaspoons seeded and minced jalapeño

1 teaspoon pure maple syrup

¼ cup extra-virgin olive oil

Fine sea salt and freshly ground black pepper

TOFU

½ cup almond flour

¼ cup nutritional yeast flakes

1 teaspoon granulated garlic or garlic powder

1 teaspoon chili powder

½ teaspoon fine sea salt

2 large eggs

One 14-ounce package extra-firm tofu, drained and pressed to remove excess moisture (see Note, page 50)

Extra-virgin olive oil, as needed

To make the chimichurri: Pulse the cilantro, lime juice, garlic, jalapeño, and maple syrup in a food processor until the cilantro is finely chopped. With the machine running, pour the oil in through the tube and process until the chimichurri is smooth. If necessary, add water, a tablespoon at a time, to give it a sauce-like consistency. Season to taste with salt and pepper. Transfer the chimichurri to a bowl and let stand while preparing the tofu.

To make the tofu: Position a rack in the center of the oven and preheat the oven to 400°F.

Mix the almond flour, nutritional yeast, granulated garlic, chili powder, and salt together in a wide, shallow dish. Beat the eggs together in a second dish. Cut the tofu vertically into eight equal slices. Dip each tofu slice in the eggs to coat, letting the excess egg drip back into

(recipe continues)

the dish. Coat the tofu in the almond mixture, gently patting the coating to adhere. (If you reserve one hand for dipping the tofu in the egg, and the other hand for coating with the almond flour, you will avoid coating your fingers with the almond mixture.) Transfer to a platter and let stand for about 10 minutes to help the coating set.

Lightly oil a large rimmed baking sheet. Place the baking sheet in the oven and let it heat until it is very hot, about 3 minutes. Remove the baking sheet from the oven and arrange the tofu on the sheet. Return to the oven and bake until the crusted undersides are golden, about 12 minutes. Flip the tofu over and continue baking until the crust is golden brown, about 12 minutes more.

Transfer two tofu slices to each dinner plate. Drizzle each with about 2 tablespoons of the chimichurri and serve.

Lentil loaf was a fairly regular dinner item when the kids were little. It's wonderfully nourishing, with a hearty texture. I've updated it over the years with fresh herbs and a bit of tomato flavor.

LENTIL and MUSHROOM LOAF

MAKES 6 TO 8 SERVINGS

2 tablespoons extra-virgin olive oil, plus more for the baking pan

1 medium yellow onion, chopped

1 large celery rib, cut into ¼-inch dice

10 ounces cremini mushrooms, finely chopped

2 garlic cloves, minced

1½ cups boiling water

3 tablespoons ground flaxseeds

2 tablespoons tomato paste

2 cups cooked lentils (see Basic Cooked Beans, page 276), or use drained canned lentils

1 cup Basic Brown Rice (page 275)

¾ cup old-fashioned rolled oats

½ cup finely chopped walnuts

2 tablespoons tamari or soy sauce

2 tablespoons nutritional yeast flakes

¼ cup coarsely chopped fresh basil

1 teaspoon finely chopped fresh thyme

1 teaspoon ground cumin

1 teaspoon pure maple syrup

1 teaspoon fine sea salt

½ teaspoon freshly ground black pepper

Position a rack in the center of the oven and preheat the oven to 350°F. Lightly oil a 9 by 5-inch loaf pan.

Heat the oil in a large skillet over medium-high heat. Add the onion and celery and cook, stirring occasionally, until the onion softens, about 2 minutes. Stir in the mushrooms and cook, stirring occasionally, until they are lightly browned, about 8 minutes. Stir in the garlic and cook until it is fragrant, about 1 minute. Transfer the mushroom mixture to a large bowl.

Mix ½ cup of the boiling water with the flaxseeds in a small bowl—the mixture will become a thick paste. Whisk the remaining 1 cup boiling water with the tomato paste in the measuring cup to dissolve the tomato paste.

(recipe continues)

Add the flaxseeds and tomato paste mixtures to the bowl with the mushroom mixture. Add the lentils, brown rice, oats, walnuts, tamari, nutritional yeast, basil, thyme, cumin, maple syrup, salt, and pepper and mix well until the mixture is thoroughly combined. Spread evenly in the prepared loaf pan.

Bake until the top is crusty and browned and the interior looks moist, but not wet, when the top of the loaf is cut into with the tip of a dinner knife, about 1 hour. Let the loaf cool for 10 minutes. Run a knife around the interior of the loaf pan. Invert and unmold the loaf onto a platter. Slice and serve hot.

LENTILS contain high levels of soluble fiber, which can help lower cholesterol and reduce the risk of heart disease. They're also packed with protein, vitamins, and minerals.
—MEHMET

Haloumi is a Cypriot cheese, a semi-hard, unripened brined cheese made from a mixture of goat's and sheep's milk. It's delicious and is ideal for grilling. It softens without melting, forms a beautiful charred crust, and has an irresistible salty flavor that can stand up to any vegetable pairing. These kebabs are the first ones to go at any family barbecue.

GRILLED HALOUMI and VEGETABLE KEBAB

MAKES 6 SERVINGS

LEMON DRESSING

3 tablespoons fresh lemon juice

1 teaspoon dried oregano

1 garlic clove, crushed through a garlic press

½ cup extra-virgin olive oil

Fine sea salt and freshly ground black pepper

1 small fennel bulb

Two 8.8-ounce packages Haloumi cheese (see Note), cut into 18 equal pieces

3 large shallots, peeled and halved

6 large button mushrooms

6 cherry tomatoes

SPECIAL EQUIPMENT:

6 long metal or bamboo skewers (if using bamboo, soak in cold water for 30 minutes, then drain)

To make the dressing: Whisk the lemon juice, oregano, and garlic together in a small bowl. Gradually whisk in the oil. Season to taste with the salt and pepper.

Cut off the fennel stalks and fronds, if attached, from the bulb. Cut the bulb into six equal wedges. Cut out the thick central core from each wedge. Remove the inner layers so each wedge is only two or three layers thick. Reserve the inner bulbs, stalks, and fronds for another use.

Divide the cheese, the fennel wedges, the shallot halves, mushrooms, and cherry tomatoes equally among the six skewers. Place the kebabs in a single layer in a long glass or ceramic dish. Pour the dressing over the kebabs. Let stand at room temperature, occasionally spooning the dressing over the kebabs, for about 30 minutes.

Prepare an outdoor grill for direct cooking over medium (400°F) heat.

Remove the kebabs from the dressing, letting the excess dressing drip back into the dish. Reserve the dressing. Place the kebabs on the grill, with the kebabs running perpendicular to the grill grid, and close the grill lid. Cook, with the lid closed, turning once or twice, until the cheese is lightly browned and the fennel is crisp-tender, 6 to 8 minutes. Remove from the grill. Place each kebab on a dinner plate, drizzle with a spoonful of the reserved dressing, and serve.

NOTE Haloumi is almost always imported from Cyprus, where it is packed in packages of 500 grams to 1 kilo, so you won't find it sold in 1-pound portions.

Black cod is a delicate, almost buttery fish. Here, its lovely fattiness is balanced by the fresh tastes of orange and fennel and the bright, almost licorice flavor of tarragon.

BLACK COD with BRAISED FENNEL, LEEKS, and TARRAGON

MAKES 4 SERVINGS

FISH AND MARINADE

¼ cup fresh orange juice

1 tablespoon minced shallot

1 teaspoon tamari or soy sauce

1 teaspoon white wine or champagne vinegar

⅓ cup plus 1 tablespoon extra-virgin olive oil

Fine sea salt and freshly ground black pepper

4 black cod fillets (each 6 to 7 ounces and 1 inch thick)

BRAISED VEGETABLES

1 pound fennel

2 medium leeks (white and pale green parts), cut into thin rounds

1 tablespoon extra-virgin olive oil

3 medium shallots, peeled and cut into thin half-moons (¾ cup)

¼ cup fresh orange juice

Fine sea salt and freshly ground black pepper

2 teaspoons finely chopped fresh tarragon, plus fresh sprigs for garnish

To marinate the fish: Whisk the orange juice, shallot, tamari, and vinegar together in a small bowl. Gradually whisk in the ⅓ cup of oil. Season the marinade to taste with the salt and pepper. Arrange the black cod in a single layer in a glass or ceramic baking dish. Pour in the marinade and turn the fish to coat. Cover and refrigerate, turning occasionally, for 30 minutes to 1 hour, no longer.

To braise the vegetables: Cut off the fennel stalks and fronds, if attached, and save them for another use. Cut the fennel bulb in half vertically. Trim out the hard central core from each half. Cut the fennel crosswise into thin half-moons about ⅛ inch thick. You should have about 3 cups.

(recipe continues)

Put the leek rounds into a medium bowl of cold water. Separate the rounds into rings in the water and agitate them well to dislodge any dirt. Lift the leeks out of the water and transfer them to a colander, leaving the dirt in the bottom of the bowl. Pat the leeks dry with paper towels. You should have about 2 cups.

Heat the 1 tablespoon oil in a large skillet over medium heat. Add the shallots and cook, stirring occasionally, until they are tender but not browned, about 2 minutes. Add the leeks and cook, stirring often, until they soften, about 2 minutes more. Add the fennel and the orange juice and season the mixture to taste with salt and pepper. Reduce the heat to medium-low. Cook, stirring occasionally, until the fennel is tender and the orange juice has almost completely evaporated, 12 to 15 minutes. During the last few minutes, stir in the chopped tarragon. Reduce the heat to very low to keep the vegetables warm.

Meanwhile, heat the remaining tablespoon oil in a large nonstick skillet over medium-high heat. Remove the cod from the marinade and shake off the excess marinade. Add the cod to the skillet, flesh side down, and cover the skillet. Cook until the fish is nicely browned, 3 to 4 minutes. Turn the fish over and cook, with the lid ajar, until the fish is barely opaque when pierced in the thickest part with the tip of a small sharp knife, 3 to 4 minutes more.

Divide the vegetables among four dinner plates. Top each with a fillet, garnish with a tarragon sprig, and serve hot.

FENNEL is commonly used to ease digestive problems, including bloating, flatulence, heartburn, and constipation. It is also useful in treating upper respiratory disorders, as it is a natural expectorant, helping the body to get rid of excess phlegm. —MEHMET

We have this only as an occasional treat because it's fried and a bit labor intensive, but if the kids had their way it would be dinner every night.

CORNBREAD-CRUSTED CALAMARI with CHIVE-YOGURT DIP

MAKES 4 TO 6 SERVINGS

CHIVE-YOGURT DIP

One 7-ounce container plain Greek yogurt (3/4 cup plus 2 tablespoons)

2 tablespoons finely chopped fresh chives

1 tablespoon hot pepper sauce

2 teaspoons fresh lemon juice

1 teaspoon pure maple syrup

Pinch of fine sea salt

CALAMARI

2 1/4 cups yellow cornmeal, preferably stone-ground

1 1/2 teaspoons organic sugar

1 1/2 teaspoons dried oregano

1 1/2 teaspoons garlic salt

1/2 teaspoon red pepper flakes

3 large eggs

1 1/2 pounds cleaned calamari, bodies (sacs) only, cut crosswise into 1/4-inch rings

Coconut oil, for frying

To make the dip: Whisk the yogurt, 2 tablespoons water, the chives, hot pepper sauce, lemon juice, maple syrup, and salt together in a small bowl. Divide the yogurt mixture equally among four to six ramekins for dipping. Set aside while cooking the calamari.

To make the calamari: Mix the cornmeal, sugar, oregano, garlic salt, and red pepper flakes together in a wide, shallow dish. Whisk the eggs together in a second shallow dish. A few at a time, dip the calamari rings in the beaten egg, letting the excess drip off, and roll them in the cornmeal mixture to coat. Transfer to a large rimmed baking sheet. Let the calamari stand at room temperature for about 15 minutes to help set the coating.

Position a rack in the center of the oven and preheat the oven to 200°F. Line a second baking sheet with paper towels.

(recipe continues)

Melt enough coconut oil (about 1 cup) in a large, deep skillet over medium-high heat to come about ⅛ inch up the sides of the skillet. Heat until the oil is shimmering but not smoking. Working in batches, without crowding, add the calamari to the skillet and cook, turning once, until golden brown, 1 to 1½ minutes. Using a slotted spoon, transfer the calamari to the lined baking sheet and keep warm in the oven while frying the rest.

Serve warm with the dip.

Oliver loves fishing and makes sure he has a hook and line whenever we are near a large body of water. He has reeled in his own dinner off the Turkish coast and on the Jersey shore, but his best catch ever was wild salmon in Alaska. This recipe, with its splash of citrus and honey, beautifully balances the oiliness of the fish.

MARINATED SALMON with SCALLIONS, LEMON, and TAMARI

MAKES 4 SERVINGS

2 scallions (white and green parts), finely chopped (⅓ cup)

¼ cup extra-virgin olive oil, plus more for the pan

1 tablespoon fresh lemon juice

1 tablespoon honey

1 teaspoon tamari

2 garlic cloves, minced

4 salmon fillets with skin (each about 6 inches long)

Fine sea salt and freshly ground black pepper

Position a rack in the center of the oven and preheat the oven to 400°F.

Whisk the scallions, oil, lemon juice, honey, tamari, and garlic together in a small bowl. Pour the marinade into a 1-gallon self-sealing plastic bag. Add the salmon and turn to coat with the marinade. Let the salmon stand at room temperature for 15 to 30 minutes.

Remove the salmon from the marinade and arrange them skin side up in an ovenproof pan or baking dish large enough to hold the salmon in a single layer. Using a slotted spoon, scatter the scallions and garlic from the marinade over the salmon. Season the fillets with salt and pepper. Bake just until opaque with a rosy center when flaked in the thickest part with the tip of a knife, about 15 minutes for rare.

Using a thin metal spatula, transfer the fillets to dinner plates and serve.

This entrée is derived from the Cajun classic, blackened redfish. (The secret ingredient in my version is a pinch of cinnamon.) The slightly sweet mango salsa is a good counterpoint to the snapper's spicy seasoning.

SPICE-CRUSTED RED SNAPPER with MANGO SALSA

MAKES 4 SERVINGS

MANGO SALSA

1 ripe mango, cut into 1/2-inch dice

1/4 cup finely chopped shallots

2 tablespoons finely chopped red bell pepper

2 tablespoons minced fresh cilantro

1 tablespoon fresh lime juice

1 teaspoon seeded and minced jalapeño

1 teaspoon champagne or white wine vinegar

1 teaspoon pure maple syrup

Fine sea salt

RED SNAPPER

1 1/2 teaspoons sweet paprika

3/4 teaspoon fine sea salt

1/2 teaspoon granulated garlic or garlic powder

1/2 teaspoon granulated onion or onion powder

1/2 teaspoon dried oregano

1/2 teaspoon dried thyme

1/2 teaspoon freshly ground black pepper

1/8 teaspoon cayenne pepper

Pinch of ground cinnamon

4 red snapper fillets with skin (about 6 ounces each)

1 tablespoon extra-virgin olive oil

To make the salsa: Combine the mango, shallots, bell pepper, cilantro, lime juice, jalapeño, vinegar, and maple syrup in a medium serving bowl. Season to taste with salt. Set the salsa aside.

To cook the snapper: Whisk the paprika, salt, garlic, onion, oregano, thyme, black and cayenne peppers, and the cinnamon together in a bowl. Season the snapper on the flesh side only with the spice mixture.

Heat the oil in a large nonstick skillet over medium-high heat until the oil is very hot but not smoking. Add the snapper fillets, seasoned side down, and cook until browned, about 3 minutes. Flip the snapper, reduce the heat to medium, and cover. Cook until the fish is barely opaque when flaked in the thickest part, about 5 minutes.

Serve with the salsa passed on the side.

This mild-flavored trout is baked with a bold coating of horseradish, garlic, and capers for a dish that is ridiculously easy to make but is actually quite elegant in its simplicity. I serve it with a side of asparagus or puréed cauliflower for a light dinner.

BAKED TROUT FILLETS with HORSERADISH-CAPER GLAZE

MAKES 4 SERVINGS

2 tablespoons extra-virgin olive oil, plus more for the baking dish

1 tablespoon fresh lemon juice

1 tablespoon drained nonpareil capers

1 tablespoon finely chopped fresh chives

2 teaspoons drained prepared horseradish

1 teaspoon Dijon mustard

1 teaspoon honey

1 garlic clove, pressed through a garlic press

Fine sea salt and freshly ground black pepper

4 rainbow trout fillets

Position a rack in the top third of the oven and preheat the oven to 400°F. Lightly oil a 9 by 13-inch baking dish or cast-iron skillet.

Using a fork, mix the oil, lemon juice, capers, chives, horseradish, mustard, honey, and garlic together in a small bowl until combined. Season to taste with salt and pepper.

Arrange the trout fillets, skin side down, next to each other in the baking dish. Spread each with the horseradish mixture. Bake until the fish looks barely opaque when flaked in the thickest part with the tip of a small sharp knife, 15 to 20 minutes. Serve hot.

TROUT Salmon gets all the glory, but we like to mix it up with trout, which can help to restore moisture to your skin by fortifying the ceramide barrier, resulting in healthier skin. —**MEHMET**

I love this cauliflower purée as an alternative to carb-heavy mashed potatoes. It's flavorful enough to eat on its own, but subtle enough to make a nice bed for a seafood.

The key to preparing the scallops is sautéing them in a hot skillet to give them a beautiful golden surface. Make sure to ask your fishmonger for "dry" scallops (which means that they haven't been saturated in preservatives), because the typical "wet" scallops give off so much of their soaking liquid that they never brown properly.

SEARED SCALLOPS with CAULIFLOWER and GARLIC PURÉE

MAKES 4 SERVINGS

CAULIFLOWER AND GARLIC PURÉE

1 head cauliflower (about 2½ pounds), cut into florets

12 large garlic cloves, smashed under the flat side of a knife and peeled

2 tablespoons unsalted butter

¼ to ½ cup whole milk, heated to steaming

Fine sea salt and freshly ground white or black pepper

SCALLOPS

12 large, plump sea scallops, patted dry on paper towels

Fine sea salt and freshly ground black pepper

2 tablespoons coconut oil

2 tablespoons unsalted butter

2 tablespoons fresh lemon juice

2 tablespoons finely chopped fresh chives, plus more for garnish

To make the purée: Bring a large saucepan of salted water to a boil over high heat. Add the cauliflower and garlic. Reduce the heat to medium-low and cover the saucepan with the lid ajar. Cook at a brisk simmer until the cauliflower is tender, 12 to 15 minutes. Drain well.

Return the cauliflower and garlic to the saucepan. Cook over low heat, stirring often, to evaporate excess moisture, about 2 minutes. Remove from the heat. Add the butter and ¼ cup of the milk to the saucepan. Using an immersion blender, process the vegetable mixture, adding more milk as needed to make a smooth purée. Season to taste with salt and pepper. Return the saucepan to very low heat. Cover the saucepan with the lid ajar to keep the purée warm.

To cook the scallops: Season the scallops all over with the salt and pepper. Melt the oil in a large nonstick skillet over medium-high heat until the oil is very hot. Place the scallops in the skillet, flat sides down. Cook until the undersides are golden brown, about 3 minutes. Using kitchen tongs, flip the scallops and cook until the other sides are golden brown and the scallops are barely opaque when pierced in the center with the tip of a small, sharp knife, about 3 minutes more. (If you like scallops well cooked, cover the skillet during the last 3 minutes of cooking.) Transfer the scallops to a plate.

Reduce the heat to very low. Add the butter and lemon juice and stir with a wooden spoon, scraping up the browned bits in the skillet, just until the butter has melted and melded with the juice into a sauce. Stir in the chives.

Spoon equal amounts of the purée into four shallow bowls. Top each with three scallops, and drizzle the scallops with the sauce. Sprinkle with more chives and serve.

You know those days when you don't have time to run to the market, so you're left staring into the freezer wondering what you've got hiding in the way back? Recently, for me there was just shrimp, corn, and edamame! Thankfully, in the pantry, I had a trusty can of Old Bay Seasoning just waiting to transform a last-minute dinner into a virtual beach party.

OLD BAY SHRIMP with EDAMAME SUCCOTASH

MAKES 4 SERVINGS

SUCCOTASH

1 tablespoon extra-virgin olive oil

1/2 large red bell pepper, cored and cut into 1/2-inch dice

2 tablespoons finely chopped shallots

1 garlic clove, minced

1 1/2 cups fresh or thawed frozen corn kernels (cut from about 2 ears)

1 cup thawed frozen shelled edamame

1 tablespoon fresh lime juice

Fine sea salt and freshly ground black pepper

SHRIMP

2 pounds jumbo shrimp (21–25 count), peeled and deveined

1 tablespoon extra-virgin olive oil

1 tablespoon Old Bay Seasoning

2 tablespoons finely chopped fresh chives, for garnish

Lime wedges, for serving

To make the succotash: Heat the oil in a large skillet over medium heat. Add the bell pepper and cook until it has softened, about 3 minutes. Add the shallots and garlic and cook, stirring occasionally, until the shallots soften, about 1 minute. Add the corn and edamame and cook until they are heated through, about 5 minutes. Remove from the heat. Stir in the lime juice and season to taste with the salt and pepper.

Position a broiler rack about 6 inches from the heat and preheat the broiler on high.

To make the shrimp: Toss the shrimp and oil in a large bowl. Sprinkle with the Old Bay Seasoning and toss again. Spread the shrimp on a broiler pan. Broil, without turning, until the shrimp turn opaque, about 3 minutes.

Divide the shrimp and succotash among four dinner plates, sprinkle with the chives, and serve with the lime wedges.

Peanut butter is one of those ingredients that just seems to go with everything. (Think about it: Ice cream? Check. Bananas? Check. Noodles? Check. Tomatoes? Okay, probably not—but it *is* remarkably versatile.) Here, peanut butter is combined with Sriracha and coconut to give these chicken breasts some smooth, tropical heat.

COCONUT-CRUSTED CHICKEN BREASTS with PEANUT SRIRACHA DIP

MAKES 4 SERVINGS

DIP

¼ cup smooth or chunky natural-style peanut butter

¼ cup light coconut milk or whole milk

2 tablespoons fresh lime juice

1 tablespoon finely chopped shallot

2 teaspoons tamari or soy sauce

1 teaspoon peeled and finely shredded fresh ginger (use the small holes on a box grater)

1 teaspoon Sriracha or Chinese chili-garlic sauce

1 garlic clove, crushed through a garlic press

CHICKEN

4 skinless, boneless chicken breast halves (each about 6 ounces)

1 teaspoon granulated garlic or garlic powder

1 teaspoon granulated onion or onion powder

1 teaspoon fine sea salt

½ teaspoon freshly ground black pepper

½ cup unbleached all-purpose flour

2 large eggs

½ cup unsweetened shredded coconut (not desiccated coconut)

½ cup panko (Japanese bread crumbs)

3 tablespoons coconut oil

To make the dip: Whisk all of the ingredients together in a medium bowl, adding about 2 tablespoons water, as needed, to thin the mixture to dip consistency. Set the dip aside while preparing the chicken.

To prepare the chicken: One at a time, place a chicken breast half between two sheets of plastic wrap. Using a flat meat pounder or a rolling pin, pound the chicken until it is about ½ inch thick. Mix the granulated garlic, granulated onion, salt, and pepper in a small bowl. Season the chicken all over with the garlic mixture.

Spread the flour in a wide, shallow dish. Beat the eggs together in a second dish. Mix the coconut and bread crumbs together in a third dish. One at a time, coat a chicken breast in the flour. Transfer it to the beaten egg, and turn to coat it, letting the excess egg drip back into the dish. Add to the bread-crumb mixture and turn to coat, gently patting the mixture on the chicken to adhere. Transfer the chicken to a platter and let stand for about 10 minutes to help the coating set.

Melt the coconut oil in a large nonstick skillet over medium heat until the oil is hot but not smoking. Add the chicken. Cook, adjusting the heat as needed so the coating browns without burning, until the underside is golden brown and crisp, 3 to 4 minutes. Flip the chicken over and continue cooking until the other side is browned and the chicken feels firm when pressed in the center with a fingertip, about 3 minutes more. Transfer the chicken to paper towels to drain for about a minute.

Transfer the chicken to a cutting board. Cut crosswise, across the grain, into slices about ½ inch thick. Place each sliced chicken breast on a dinner plate. Pour the peanut sauce into four individual small bowls, and add to each plate for dipping the chicken. Serve immediately.

It doesn't get much easier than this! Just rub the Mediterranean seasoning on the drumsticks and pop them in the oven. They come out so delicious your family will think you spent ages slaving away in the kitchen.

ROASTED CHICKEN DRUMSTICKS
with HERB-GARLIC RUB

MAKES 4 SERVINGS

8 chicken drumsticks with skin and bone

1 tablespoon extra-virgin olive oil

2 teaspoons dried oregano

1 teaspoon garlic salt

1 teaspoon granulated onion or onion powder

½ teaspoon crumbled dried rosemary

¼ teaspoon cayenne pepper, or more to taste

Position a rack in the center of the oven and preheat the oven to 400°F.

Toss the chicken and oil together in a large bowl to coat the chicken. Mix the oregano, garlic salt, granulated onion, rosemary, and cayenne in a small bowl. Sprinkle the oregano mixture over the chicken and toss again to coat it evenly.

Arrange the chicken in a single layer in a large baking dish. Bake, turning the chicken once and basting occasionally with the pan juices, until it is golden brown and shows no sign of pink when pierced at the bone with the tip of a small, sharp knife, about 45 minutes. Serve hot.

OREGANO is high in carvacol, a potent antimicrobial compound. It's been shown to kill listeria and staphylococcus bacteria. It even fights candida to help prevent yeast infections. Lisa puts this oil on the kids when they are sick, which makes them smell like pizzas, but I prefer mine in my food. —MEHMET

Our Afghani friends introduced us to this aromatic dish with chicken. I prefer to make it with game hens instead because I like to keep the grain separate from the poultry (for the vegetarians) and because the game hens just feel special. There's something almost fancy about them on a plate. Here, they get a zesty mango chutney glaze that complements the fruit and spice in the rice.

GAME HENS with SPICED BASMATI RICE

MAKES 4 SERVINGS

GAME HENS

4 game hens (each about 1 pound), giblets removed

2 tablespoons extra-virgin olive oil

1 teaspoon garlic salt

1 teaspoon ground cumin

1/2 teaspoon freshly ground black pepper

1/2 cup mango chutney, puréed in a mini food processor or blender, if necessary

SPICED BASMATI RICE

1 1/2 teaspoons cumin seeds

2 tablespoons unsalted butter

1/3 cup finely chopped shallots

1 1/2 cups basmati rice

3 cups water, All-Purpose Vegetable Broth (page 278), or canned reduced-sodium chicken broth

One 3-inch cinnamon stick

1 1/2 teaspoons fine sea salt

1/2 cup toasted slivered almonds

1/2 cup golden raisins

1/3 cup coarsely chopped pistachios

Grated zest of 1 orange

1/2 cup water, All-Purpose Vegetable Broth (page 278), or canned reduced-sodium chicken broth

To cook the hens: Position a rack in the center of the oven and preheat the oven to 400°F.

Rub the game hens with the oil. Mix the garlic salt, ground cumin, and pepper in a small bowl, and season the hens, inside and out, with the mixture. Arrange the hens side by side on a large wire rack in a roasting pan.

Roast until an instant-read thermometer inserted in the thickest part of the breast reads 160°F, about 1 hour. Remove the pan from the oven and increase the oven temperature to 450°F. Brush the hens all over with the chutney. Return them to the oven and continue roasting

(recipe continues)

until the glaze is lightly browned, 5 to 10 minutes more. Remove the hens from the pan and let stand at room temperature for 5 minutes.

About 35 minutes before serving, make the rice: Heat a medium saucepan over medium heat. Add the cumin seeds and cook, stirring often, until fragrant and toasted, 1 to 2 minutes. Transfer the seeds to a plate.

Off the heat, add the butter to the saucepan and let it melt. Return the saucepan to medium heat and add the shallots. Cook, stirring often, until the shallots are softened but not browned, about 2 minutes. Add the rice and stir well. Pour in the 3 cups water and add the toasted cumin, the cinnamon stick, and salt. Bring the liquid to a boil over high heat. Reduce the heat to medium-low and tightly cover the saucepan. Simmer until the rice is tender and it has absorbed the liquid, about 20 minutes.

Remove the saucepan from the heat. Uncover the saucepan and add the almonds, raisins, pistachios, and orange zest, but do not stir them in. Cover and let stand for 5 minutes.

Skim off and discard the fat from the roasting pan. Place the pan over medium heat on top of the stove and cook until the juices are sizzling. Add the ½ cup water and bring to a boil, scraping up the browned bits in the pan with a wooden spoon. Remove from the heat.

For each serving, place a hen on a dinner plate. Stir the rice well, and discard the cinnamon stick. Divide the rice equally among the dinner plates. Drizzle with the pan juices and serve.

For years I tried to get away with only vegetarian alternatives to turkey during the holidays. My efforts were met with groans and last-minute phone calls to members of the extended family to please bring a turkey with them when they arrived. Now we have a turkey on holidays, but we cook the stuffing outside of the bird for the non-meat-eaters. (Technically it's not "stuffing," so here it's labeled as "dressing.") This version has a slight Mediterranean feel with the addition of fruit, nuts, and aromatic rosemary.

ROAST TURKEY with APRICOT and ROSEMARY DRESSING

MAKES 8 TO 12 SERVINGS

DRESSING

1 loaf crusty bread, such as French or Italian, sliced

2 tablespoons extra-virgin olive oil, plus more for the baking dish

6 medium celery ribs, cut into ½-inch dice

½ cup finely chopped shallots

1 garlic clove, minced

1½ cups dried apricots, cut into ½-inch dice

1½ cups toasted and coarsely chopped walnuts (6 ounces; see Note, page 162)

2 tablespoons finely chopped fresh flat-leaf parsley

1 tablespoon finely chopped fresh rosemary

2 cups All-Purpose Vegetable Broth (page 278), as needed

Fine sea salt and freshly ground black pepper

TURKEY

1 turkey with giblets (about 13 pounds)

1 small yellow onion, coarsely chopped

½ navel orange, cut into chunks

½ Granny Smith apple, cored and cut into chunks

6 sprigs fresh thyme

Fine sea salt and freshly ground black pepper

6 tablespoons unsalted butter, at room temperature

GIBLET BROTH AND GRAVY

1 tablespoon extra-virgin olive oil

1 small yellow onion, chopped

1 small celery rib with leaves, chopped

1 quart reduced-sodium chicken broth

2 sprigs fresh thyme

⅓ cup plus 1 tablespoon unbleached all-purpose flour

Fine sea salt and freshly ground black pepper

To make the dressing: Position the oven racks in the top third and center of the oven and preheat the oven to 350°F.

Spread the bread on two large rimmed baking sheets. Bake until the bread is golden brown, about 30 minutes. Let the bread cool but keep the oven turned on. Coarsely tear and crumble the bread into pieces about 1 inch square, and transfer to a large bowl.

Heat the oil in a large skillet over medium heat. Add the celery, cover, and cook, stirring occasionally, until tender, about 6 minutes. Stir in the shallots and garlic and cook, uncovered, stirring occasionally, until the shallots are tender, about 2 minutes more. Transfer to the bowl. Add the apricots, walnuts, parsley, and rosemary. Stir in enough vegetable broth to thoroughly moisten the dressing without making it wet. Season to taste with salt and pepper. Lightly oil a 9 by 13-inch baking dish and spread the dressing in the dish. Cover with aluminum foil. Refrigerate until ready to bake, up to 8 hours.

To roast the turkey: Reduce the oven temperature to 325°F. Remove the giblets and neck from the turkey. Pull the fat pads from the tail area. Cover and refrigerate the fat, giblets, and neck until ready to use. Mix the onion, orange and apple chunks, and thyme in a medium bowl and season them generously with salt and pepper. Stuff some of the onion mixture under the neck skin, and pin the neck skin to the back skin with a small metal or wooden skewer. Rub the turkey all over with the butter, followed by a generous seasoning of salt and pepper. Stuff the remaining onion mixture in the body cavity (no need to close the body cavity).

Place the turkey on a roasting rack in a large roasting pan. Cover the breast (but not the wings or legs) with

(recipe continues)

aluminum foil. Add 1 cup water and the reserved fat to the roasting pan. Roast the turkey, allowing the pan juices to evaporate and brown but adding more water if they threaten to burn, for 1 hour 45 minutes. Remove the foil and baste the breast with the pan drippings. Continue roasting, basting again after 20 minutes, until an instant-read thermometer inserted in the thickest part of the thigh (not touching a bone) reads 175°F, about 45 minutes more.

While the turkey is roasting, make the giblet broth: With a very heavy knife or a cleaver, chop the reserved turkey neck into 2-inch chunks. Heat the oil in a medium saucepan over medium-high heat. Add the giblets and neck (but not the liver) and cook, flipping them occasionally, until they are browned, 8 to 10 minutes. Stir in the onion and celery and cook until they are softened, about 2 minutes. Add the chicken broth and 2 cups water. Bring to a boil over high heat, skimming off any foam from the surface. Add the thyme and reduce the heat to low. Simmer until the broth is fully flavored, about 2 hours. Strain the broth through a wire strainer into a large bowl. Skim off any fat that rises to the surface.

When the turkey is done, transfer it to a large serving platter. Let the turkey stand, uncovered, while baking the stuffing (and other side dishes) and making the gravy, about 30 minutes. Increase the oven temperature to 350°F. Place the baking dish with the dressing in the oven and bake, covered, until the dressing is hot, about 30 minutes.

To make the gravy, pour the pan drippings from the roasting pan into a small glass bowl. Skim and reserve the clear yellow fat that rises to the top of the drippings. Measure 6 tablespoons (adding melted butter, if needed), discarding the excess fat. Pour the skimmed drippings into a 1-quart glass measuring cup. Add enough of the giblet broth to measure 4 cups combined drippings and broth.

Place the roasting pan over two burners on the stove over medium heat. Add the skimmed fat from the drippings. Sprinkle in the flour and whisk well. Whisk in the broth mixture and bring to a boil, whisking constantly. Reduce the heat to low and simmer, whisking occasionally, until the gravy has thickened and reduced slightly, about 5 minutes. Season to taste with salt and pepper. Strain the gravy through a mesh sieve into a medium bowl, and transfer it, as needed, to a gravy boat.

Carve the turkey and serve it with the dressing and gravy.

Mehmet likes his lamb seared so that it gets a crusty brown exterior with a deep crimson inside. The herbed hazelnut coating helps to seal in the juices so the meat stays succulent and tender. This is one of our favorite lamb dishes.

RACK OF LAMB with HAZELNUT and HERB CRUST

MAKES 4 SERVINGS

2 racks of lamb (each about 1 ¾ pounds), bones Frenched

Fine sea salt and freshly ground pepper

HAZELNUT CRUST

½ cup (2 ounces) skinned and finely chopped hazelnuts

2 small garlic cloves, crushed through a press

2 teaspoons minced fresh mint

1 teaspoon minced fresh oregano

1 teaspoon minced fresh rosemary

Extra-virgin olive oil

Position a rack in the center of the oven and preheat the oven to 400°F.

Trim each lamb rack of excess fat. Season the lamb all over with the salt and pepper. Let the lamb stand at room temperature for 15 to 30 minutes.

To make the crust: Mix the hazelnuts, garlic, mint, oregano, and rosemary together in a small bowl.

Heat 2 tablespoons of oil in a large ovenproof skillet over high heat. In batches, add the lamb racks, meaty side down, and holding and turning the lamb with tongs for an even sear, cook until the lamb is lightly browned, about 2 minutes. Remove from the heat. Transfer the lamb to a plate. Brush the meaty top of each rack with some oil. Sprinkle and coat the top of each rack with half of the hazelnut mixture, patting the mixture to help it adhere. Arrange the lamb, crusted side up, on a large rimmed baking sheet.

Roast until an instant-read thermometer inserted in the thickest part of a rack reads 125°F for rare, about 20 minutes. Transfer the racks to a carving board and let stand for 3 to 5 minutes. Carve each lamb rack between the bones to yield 16 chops, and serve.

This is a recipe that Oliver and John make whenever they want to bond over a "manly" steak. Daphne actually made it for them the first time, but Oliver quickly took it over and now claims it as his own.

GRILLED STEAK with "THE BOYS'" MARINADE

MAKES 4 SERVINGS

"THE BOYS'" MARINADE

⅓ cup extra-virgin olive oil

2 tablespoons honey

6 garlic cloves, minced

1 teaspoon ground cumin

1 teaspoon chili powder

1 teaspoon fine sea salt

1 teaspoon freshly ground black pepper

¼ teaspoon ground cinnamon

4 boneless rib-eye steaks (each about 12 ounces and 1 inch thick)

To make the marinade: Whisk the oil, honey, garlic, cumin, chili powder, salt, pepper, and cinnamon together in a medium bowl until combined.

Arrange the steaks in a large glass or ceramic baking dish. Pour in the marinade. Turn the steaks to coat them, spreading the marinade with a rubber spatula, if necessary. Cover with plastic wrap and refrigerate for at least 4 hours and up to 1 day. Remove from the refrigerator about 30 minutes before grilling.

Prepare an outdoor grill for two-zone cooking over high (550°F or more) heat. For a charcoal grill, let the coals burn until they are covered with white ash, and spread them on one side of the grill, leaving the other side empty. For a gas grill, preheat the grill on high, and turn one burner off.

Remove the steaks from the marinade, letting any excess marinade drip back into the dish. Put the steaks on the hot side of the grill and close the grill. Cook, with the lid closed as much as possible, turning once, but moving the steaks to the empty side of the grill if the marinade drips and causes flare-ups, until the steaks are well browned and but still feel somewhat squishy when pressed on top with your fingertip, about 8 minutes for medium-rare. (Or insert an instant-read thermometer horizontally into the center of the steak; it should read 130°F for medium-rare. But using a thermometer to determine the temperature of a hot steak, especially a thin cut, is not easy or especially accurate.) Remove the steaks from the grill and let stand for 3 to 5 minutes before serving.

SPECIAL-OCCASION DESSERTS

While this isn't a traditional Turkish dessert, it's made with typical fruits of the region. The mint adds a clean note to the mix. Serve on a hot afternoon when you want something light and refreshing.

TURKISH MELON and POMEGRANATE FRUIT SORBET

MAKES ABOUT 6 SERVINGS

1/2 cup water

1/2 cup organic sugar

1 cup coarsely chopped fresh mint

1 1/2 pounds peeled and diced ripe yellow melon, such as crenshaw or casaba (about 5 packed cups)

3/4 cup fresh orange, tangerine, or clementine juice

1/2 cup plus 1 tablespoon bottled pomegranate juice

3 tablespoons fresh lime juice

Bring the water and sugar to a boil in a small saucepan over high heat, stirring often to dissolve the sugar. Remove from the heat. Stir in the mint and let stand until completely cooled. Strain the syrup through a fine-mesh sieve, pressing hard on the mint.

Purée the melon in a food processor or blender and pour into a medium bowl. Whisk in the orange, pomegranate, and lime juices with the mint syrup. Place the bowl in a larger bowl of ice water and let stand, stirring occasionally, until well chilled, about 30 minutes. (Or cover and refrigerate the mixture to chill for at least 4 hours or overnight.)

Pour the chilled melon mixture into an ice cream maker and process according to the manufacturer's directions. Transfer the sorbet to a freezer-proof container and freeze for at least 4 hours before serving. Serve frozen.

POMEGRANATE SEEDS contain punicalagin, which has been shown to lower cholesterol and blood pressure. It also prevents blood platelets from sticking together too aggressively, thereby reducing atherosclerotic plaque.
—MEHMET

This is a super-fast and easy dessert when you're craving something sweet but don't want anything too heavy. The warm, honeyed fruit plays nicely against the cool, creamy yogurt.

GREEK YOGURT PARFAIT
with GRILLED FIGS

MAKES 4 SERVINGS

8 ripe green figs, halved lengthwise

Four 7-ounce containers plain Greek yogurt (see Note)

¾ cup coarsely chopped walnuts (3 ounces)

3 tablespoons raw, unfiltered honey

Ground cinnamon, for garnish

Position a broiler rack about 6 inches from the source of heat and preheat the broiler on high.

Lightly oil the broiler pan. Arrange the figs, cut side up, on the pan. Broil, without turning, until the fig juices are bubbling, 2 to 3 minutes.

Divide the yogurt among four dessert bowls or parfait glasses. Top with equal amounts of the figs, followed by the walnuts, a generous drizzle of honey, and a sprinkle of cinnamon. Serve immediately.

NOTE One 7-ounce container equals a scant cup of yogurt (¾ cup plus 2 tablespoons), so you can measure out the portions from a larger container, if you prefer.

FIGS have tons of fiber, boasting about 14 grams per cup, and are also rich in calcium. They serve as a prebiotic by feeding our needy intestinal bacteria. I grew up with fig trees, and was taught to choose those figs with a rich, deep color and a sweet fragrance. Don't wash them until you're ready to eat. —MEHMET

Caramel + salt = Best taste ever! This cake is a personal guilty pleasure. (Not *too* guilty—it's gluten free.) Use your preferred apple variety, as long as it holds its shape after cooking: Matsu, Golden Delicious, and Jonagold are good, but McIntosh is not. Serve the cake warm from the oven, sprinkled with a nice flaky salt.

GLUTEN-FREE APPLE-CARAMEL CAKE with FLAKY SALT

MAKES 8 SERVINGS

APPLE-CARAMEL LAYER

6 tablespoons (3/4 stick) unsalted butter, plus more for the pan

3/4 cup packed light brown sugar

1/4 cup pure maple syrup

2 baking apples (see suggestions above), peeled, cored, and cut into 1/4-inch wedges

CAKE

3/4 cup (11/2 sticks) unsalted butter, at room temperature

11/4 cups organic sugar

3 large eggs, at room temperature

11/2 teaspoons vanilla extract

11/2 cups gluten-free baking mix, such as Bob's Red Mill

1/2 cup coconut flour

2 teaspoons baking powder

1/4 teaspoon fine sea salt

2/3 cup whole milk

Flaky sea salt, such as Maldon or fleur de sel, for serving

Position a rack in the center of the oven and preheat the oven to 350°F. Lightly butter a 9 by 2-inch round cake pan.

To make the apple-caramel layer: Melt the butter in a medium skillet. Add the brown sugar and maple syrup and cook, stirring often, until the sugar has melted and the mixture is boiling. Pour the mixture into the prepared pan. Carefully arrange the apples in two concentric circles in the syrup, overlapping them as needed.

To make the cake: Beat the butter in a medium bowl with a hand-held electric mixer on high speed until creamy, about 1 minute. Gradually beat in the sugar and continue mixing, scraping down the sides of the bowl as

(recipe continues)

needed, until the mixture is light in color and texture, about 2 minutes. One at a time, beat in the eggs, beating well after each addition, followed by the vanilla.

Whisk the baking mix, coconut flour, baking powder, and fine sea salt together in another medium bowl. With the mixer on low speed, add the flour mixture to the butter mixture in thirds, alternating with two additions of the milk, mixing just until combined after each addition. Scrape the batter into the cake pan and smooth the top.

Bake until the cake springs back when pressed lightly in the center, 35 to 40 minutes. Let the cake cool in the pan on a wire cooling rack for 10 minutes. Run a knife around the inside edge of the pan. Place a serving plate over the cake pan. Holding the pan and plate together with a kitchen towel to protect your hands, invert them to unmold the cake. Remove the pan. Cut the cake into wedges and serve, sprinkling flaky salt to taste over each serving.

APPLES Rich in soluble fiber and flavonoids like quercetin, apples have been shown to lower cholesterol, stabilize blood sugar levels, and boost the immune system. Many of the apple's phytonutrients are in the skin, so eat them unpeeled for maximum benefit. —MEHMET

This cake is so utterly delectable that you'll love it whether or not you're a vegan. The secret is cooked carrot purée, which keeps the cake extra moist. Because it's so rich, we make this as a sheet cake and opt for smaller pieces, but if you want to serve it as a layered birthday cake, double the recipe and bake in two 9-inch round cake pans for about 25 minutes. (You'll need to double the frosting, too.)

CARROT CAKE
with CASHEW FROSTING

MAKES 9 SERVINGS

CASHEW FROSTING

1½ cups unsalted and unroasted whole cashews (6 ounces)

½ cup confectioners' sugar

2 tablespoons coconut oil

2 teaspoons vanilla extract

2 teaspoons fresh lemon juice

¼ teaspoon fine sea salt

⅓ cup coconut milk, as needed

CARROT CAKE

2 cups shredded carrots (use the large holes of a box grater)

1 cup packed light brown sugar

½ cup coconut oil

½ cup coconut milk

1 teaspoon vanilla extract

¾ cup unbleached all-purpose flour

¾ cup whole wheat flour

1½ teaspoons ground cinnamon

1 teaspoon baking powder

½ teaspoon baking soda

½ teaspoon ground allspice

½ teaspoon fine sea salt

½ cup finely chopped walnuts (2 ounces)

Grated zest of 1 orange

To begin the frosting: Put the cashews in a large bowl and add enough water to cover them by 1 inch. Let them stand until softened, at least 2 and up to 4 hours. Drain well.

To make the cake: Put 1 cup of the shredded carrots in a medium saucepan. Add enough cold water to barely cover the carrots and bring to a boil over high heat. Reduce the heat to medium low and simmer until the carrots are tender, about 10 minutes. Drain well. Purée the carrots in

(recipe continues)

a mini food processor or blender. You should have ⅓ cup purée.

Position a rack in the center of the oven and preheat the oven to 350°F. Lightly and evenly coat the inside of an 8-inch square baking pan with solid coconut oil. Dust with flour and tap out the excess flour.

Beat the brown sugar and coconut oil with an electric hand mixer at high speed until slightly paler in color, about 1 minute. Add the coconut milk, vanilla, and the carrot purée and beat until foamy, about 1 minute more. Whisk the all-purpose and whole wheat flours, cinnamon, baking powder, baking soda, allspice, and salt together in a large bowl, being sure to break up any baking soda clumps. Pour in the brown sugar mixture and mix just until combined into a thick batter. Stir in the remaining 1 cup shredded carrots with the walnuts and orange zest. Spread the batter evenly in the cake pan.

Bake until the cake springs back when pressed gently in the center with a fingertip, about 35 minutes. Let cool completely in the pan on a wire cake rack.

To complete the frosting: Transfer the drained cashews to a food processor. Add the confectioners' sugar, coconut oil, vanilla, lemon juice, and salt, and pulse until the nuts are finely chopped. With the machine running, and occasionally stopping to scrape down the sides of the work bowl, add enough of the coconut milk to make a smooth, spreadable frosting. Spread the frosting over the top of the cake. Cut into squares and serve.

CASHEWS are full of healthy monounsaturated fats and amino acids, including L-tryptophan, which increases serotonin in the body. They also help fight cancer with the tumor-starving flavonoid proanthocyanidin. —MEHMET

The only thing Mehmet asks for on his birthday is this ultra-decadent chocolate cake. (Oh, don't look so shocked! He just eats one piece and it's only once a year.) The first time I made it for him was over thirty years ago, with my friend Marilyn. The recipe has evolved from her classic version to a darker chocolate cake, but it's still got that sticky-sweet-gooey coconut icing.

ALMOST GERMAN CHOCOLATE CAKE

MAKES 10 TO 12 SERVINGS

DARK CHOCOLATE CAKE

1 cup boiling water

3/4 cup natural or Dutch-processed unsweetened cocoa powder

2/3 cup plain Greek yogurt

2/3 cup whole milk

1/2 teaspoon cider vinegar

10 tablespoons (1¼ sticks) unsalted butter, at room temperature

2 cups organic sugar

3 large eggs, at room temperature

1 teaspoon vanilla extract

1¾ cups unbleached all-purpose flour

1½ teaspoons baking soda

1/4 teaspoon fine sea salt

COCONUT-PECAN ICING

1/2 cup (1 stick) unsalted butter, cut into tablespoons

Two 14-ounce cans non-GMO condensed milk

6 large egg yolks

2 cups unsweetened shredded coconut

2 cups coarsely chopped pecans or walnuts (8 ounces)

2 teaspoons vanilla extract

1/8 teaspoon fine sea salt

To make the cake: Whisk the boiling water and cocoa together in a medium bowl to dissolve the cocoa. Refrigerate, whisking often, until the mixture has cooled completely.

Whisk the yogurt, milk, and vinegar together in a glass measuring cup, and set aside at room temperature while the cocoa mixture is cooling.

Position a rack in the center of the oven and preheat the oven to 350°F. Lightly butter two 9-inch pans and line the bottoms with wax or parchment paper. Dust the sides of the pans with flour and tap out the excess flour.

(recipe continues)

Beat the butter in a medium bowl with a hand-held electric mixer on high speed until creamy, about 1 minute. Gradually beat in the sugar and continue mixing until the mixture is light in color and texture, about 2 minutes. One at a time, beat in the eggs, followed by the vanilla and the cooled cocoa mixture.

Whisk the flour, baking soda, and salt together in another medium bowl. With the mixer on low speed, add the flour mixture to the butter mixture in thirds, alternating with two additions of the yogurt mixture, mixing just until combined after each addition. Scrape the batter into the cake pans and smooth the top.

Bake until a wooden toothpick inserted into the center of the cakes comes out clean, about 35 minutes. Let the cakes cool in the pans on a wire cooling rack for 10 minutes. Run a knife around the inside edge of each pan. Invert the pans onto the rack to unmold the cakes. Flip the cakes, right side up, and let cool completely.

To make the icing: Melt the butter in a medium, heavy-bottomed saucepan over medium heat. Stir in the condensed milk and cook, stirring often, until the mixture is simmering. Whisk the egg yolks together in a medium bowl. Gradually beat in about a cup of the hot condensed milk mixture, and pour this back into the saucepan. Cook, stirring constantly, until the mixture returns to a simmer and thickens. Transfer the mixture to a large bowl. Stir in the coconut, pecans, vanilla, and salt. Let the icing cool for a few minutes until it is thick enough to spread.

Place a cake layer, flat side facing up, on a serving plate. Spread it with about ¾ cup of the icing. Top with the second cake layer, flat side down. Spread the top, and then the sides, with the remaining icing. Let the icing cool completely. (The cake can be stored at room temperature for up to 1 day.) Slice and serve.

Our quintessential fall activity is pumpkin picking. Every October, just before Halloween, the whole family piles into the minivan and heads to a "pick-your-own" farm in upstate New York. When we have selected the fattest, smoothest, heaviest specimens, we return home and spend the rest of the afternoon baking pies and carving jack-o'-lanterns. If you can't make it to a pumpkin patch, you can use another winter squash variety for this recipe.

FRESH PUMPKIN PIE
with COOKIE DOUGH CRUST

MAKES 8 SERVINGS

PIE DOUGH

1¼ cups unbleached all-purpose flour, plus more for shaping and rolling out the dough

3 tablespoons organic sugar

⅛ teaspoon fine sea salt

½ cup (1 stick) cold unsalted butter, cut into ½-inch cubes

2 large egg yolks

3 tablespoons ice water

FILLING

1 sweet or cheese pumpkin, or butternut squash (about 2¼ pounds)

One 14-ounce can non-GMO condensed milk

2 large eggs, beaten

1½ teaspoons ground cinnamon

1 teaspoon ground cardamom

½ teaspoon ground allspice

1 teaspoon vanilla extract

½ teaspoon ground ginger

To make the pie dough: Mix the flour, sugar, and salt together in a medium bowl. Add the butter and mix to coat the butter with the flour mixture. Using your fingertips, quickly rub the butter into the flour mixture until it resembles coarse meal. (Or, instead of your fingertips, use a pastry blender.) Stir the yolks and ice water together in a small bowl. Using a fork, add and stir in enough of the yolk mixture until the dough clumps together. Turn the dough out onto a lightly floured work surface and knead a few times until it is smooth. Shape the dough into a thick disk and wrap in plastic wrap. Refrigerate until the dough is chilled but not hard, 1 to 2 hours.

(recipe continues)

Begin the filling: If you're carving a jack-o'-lantern, cut off the top of the pumpkin to make a lid, then use a large spoon to scrape enough of the inner flesh to measure 6 packed cups, leaving the shell intact. If you are just making pie, cut the pumpkin into quarters and scrape out the seeds. Using a sturdy vegetable peeler, peel the pumpkin, and cut the flesh into chunks about 1½ inches square. Place the chunks (or scraped-out flesh) into a large saucepan and add enough cold water to barely cover them. Bring to a boil over high heat. Reduce the heat to medium-low and cover. Simmer until the pumpkin is tender, 15 to 20 minutes. Drain the pumpkin well in a wire sieve. Using a spatula, firmly press the pumpkin to extract excess moisture. Once the pumpkin has cooled, transfer it to a blender and purée until smooth with a thickness similar to canned pumpkin; 2 pounds of pumpkin should yield about 2 cups of purée.

Position a rack in the bottom third of the oven and preheat the oven to 400°F. Place a large rimmed baking sheet on the rack to heat.

Unwrap the dough. On a lightly floured work surface, roll out the dough into a 12- to 13-inch round about ⅛ inch thick. Transfer the dough to a 9-inch pie pan. If the dough breaks, just patch it together. Fold the dough itself under so the edge of the fold is flush with the edge of the pan. Flute the dough. Refrigerate the dough-lined pan to chill for 20 to 30 minutes.

Whisk the cooled pumpkin, condensed milk, eggs, cinnamon, cardamom, allspice, vanilla, and ginger together. Pour the filling into the dough-lined pan and place on the hot baking sheet. Bake for 15 minutes. Reduce the temperature to 350°F. Continue baking until a knife inserted into the center of the filling comes out clean, about 35 minutes. Transfer to a wire cooling rack and let cool. Cut into wedges and serve.

PUMPKINS are a great source of beta-carotene, a potent antioxidant. Your body converts carotenes into vitamin A, which is essential for eye health and a strong and healthy immune system. Pumpkins also contain zinc, a powerful immunity enhancer. —MEHMET

Oliver is crazy about this fresh, fruity pie. (Don't tell him it's both vegan and gluten free.) The creamy (but cream-less) filling is made from silken tofu, and the flourless crust is a delicious combination of ground walnuts, dates, and thyme. Be sure to use moist dates, such as Medjool. They can be pitted, but the prechopped variety is too dry.

LEMON and BLUEBERRY PIE

MAKES 8 SERVINGS

WALNUT-DATE CRUST

1½ cups coarsely chopped walnuts (6 ounces)

¾ cup pitted and coarsely chopped moist dates, such as Medjool

2 teaspoons finely chopped fresh thyme

1 teaspoon vanilla extract

FILLING

1 pound silken tofu, drained on paper towels

½ cup organic sugar

Finely grated zest of 1 lemon

¼ cup fresh lemon juice

2 tablespoons cornstarch

Pinch of fine sea salt

1 teaspoon vanilla extract

One 6-ounce container fresh blueberries (about 1⅓ cups), plus more for garnish

Position a rack in the center of the oven and preheat the oven to 350°F. Coat the inside of a 9-inch pie pan with some coconut oil.

To make the crust: Pulse the walnuts, dates, thyme, and vanilla together in a food processor until the walnuts are very finely chopped and the mixture holds together when pressed. (Or process the ingredients in batches in a blender.) Press the walnut mixture firmly and evenly into the pie pan. Place the pan on a baking sheet.

Bake the crust until it begins to brown around the edges, 12 to 15 minutes. Remove from the oven and let cool.

To make the filling: Process the tofu, sugar, lemon zest and juice, cornstarch, and salt together in the food processor (or blender) until smooth. Transfer the mixture to a medium saucepan. Cook over medium heat, stirring almost constantly, until the mixture comes to a full boil and is lightly thickened. Remove from the heat and stir in the vanilla. Let the filling cool slightly.

Sprinkle the blueberries evenly in the pie pan. Pour the tofu cream evenly over the blueberries and garnish with a few more blueberries. Refrigerate, uncovered, until the filling is chilled and set, at least 2 hours or overnight. Slice the pie and serve it chilled.

BLUEBERRIES One serving of this superfood has more antioxidant activity than almost any other fruit or vegetable, which is why we call them "brain berries" on the show. Antioxidants fight the free radicals that cause aging problems that range from wrinkles to dementia.
—MEHMET

There are three foods that epitomize our summers in Maine: lobster rolls, blueberry pancakes, and rhubarb crumble. This gluten-free version is my homage to the last, which was introduced to us by our dear friend Martha, the rhubarb maven. Rhubarb is naturally tart, so you may be tempted to overcompensate with lots of extra sugar. Resist. The 1/2 cup I use here is plenty when combined with the sweet strawberries.

MAINE RHUBARB-STRAWBERRY CRUMBLE

MAKES 6 SERVINGS

TOPPING

1 cup gluten-free old-fashioned rolled oats

2/3 cup almond flour

2/3 cup chopped walnuts (about 2 1/2 ounces)

Pinch of fine sea salt

1/3 cup Sucanat (brown dehydrated cane sugar)

6 tablespoons (3/4 stick) unsalted butter, cut into tablespoons, at room temperature

1 teaspoon vanilla extract

FILLING

1 1/2 pounds trimmed rhubarb

1/2 cup Sucanat (brown dehydrated cane sugar)

2 tablespoons cornstarch

2 tablespoons unsalted butter

1 pound (or about 1 1/2 dry pints) strawberries, hulled and halved

1 tablespoon fresh lemon juice

Finely grated zest of 1/2 orange

Position a rack in the center of the oven and preheat the oven to 400°F. Lightly butter a glass or ceramic 9½-inch deep-dish pie pan.

To make the topping: Combine the oats, almond flour, walnuts, salt, and Sucanat in a medium bowl. Add the butter. Using your fingertips, work the butter into the oat mixture until it is homogeneous. Add the vanilla and work it in.

(recipe continues)

To make the filling: If the rhubarb stalks are wider than 1 inch, cut them in half lengthwise. Cut the rhubarb crosswise into ¾-inch slices. Mix the Sucanat and cornstarch together in a small bowl. (Do not skip this step, or the cornstarch will clump when brought to a simmer.)

Melt the butter in a large skillet over medium heat. Add the rhubarb and cook, stirring occasionally, until it begins to soften, about 5 minutes. Add the strawberries, ½ cup water, the sugar mixture, the lemon juice, and orange zest and stir well. Bring the mixture just to a simmer.

Pour the filling into the pie pan. Crumble the topping over the filling. Place the pie pan on a large rimmed baking sheet to catch any drips. Bake until the filling is bubbling and the topping is crisp, about 40 minutes. Let cool for at least 30 minutes. Serve warm.

When I was growing up, these cookies signaled the arrival of fall. They were spicy and crisp, and they went beautifully with a glass of fresh-pressed cider. They also made me feel somehow . . . mature, like I wasn't eating "kids' food." I still enjoy them now that I'm an adult, but these days I prefer to make them gluten free.

GINGER SNAP COOKIES

MAKES ABOUT 2½ DOZEN COOKIES

4 tablespoons (½ stick) unsalted butter, at room temperature

½ cup organic sugar

1 large egg, at room temperature

¼ cup unsulfured molasses

¼ cup pure maple syrup

2 cups gluten-free baking mix, such as Bob's Red Mill

2 teaspoons baking soda

1 teaspoon ground ginger

1 teaspoon ground cinnamon

¼ teaspoon fine sea salt

Position the racks in the top third and center of the oven and preheat the oven to 350°F. Line two large baking sheets with parchment paper.

Beat the butter and sugar together in a medium bowl with an electric hand mixer set on high speed until the mixture is pale, about 2 minutes. Beat in the egg, followed by the molasses and syrup.

Whisk the baking mix, baking soda, ginger, cinnamon, and salt together in another medium bowl. Gradually stir this into the butter mixture to make a soft dough.

Using a level tablespoon for each, shape the dough into rough balls and drop them onto the prepared baking sheets about 1½ inches apart. Bake, switching the position of the sheets from top to bottom and front to back halfway through baking, until the tops of the cookies look dry and set, about 15 minutes. Let the cookies cool on the baking sheets for 3 minutes. Transfer the cookies to wire cooling racks and let cool completely. Repeat with the remaining dough on cooled and lined baking sheets.

CINNAMON lowers blood sugar levels by helping insulin work more effectively in the liver. Studies have shown that it can also help reduce high LDL cholesterol levels, particularly in people with Type 2 diabetes. —MEHMET

Oliver says these chewy morsels remind him of his favorite candy bar (hint: it's got coconut, dark chocolate, and almonds), but he admits he likes these even better.

CHOCOLATE ALMOND MACAROONS

MAKES ABOUT 32 COOKIES

MACAROONS

4 cups unsweetened shredded (not desiccated) coconut

One 14-ounce can non-GMO condensed milk

1 teaspoon vanilla extract

¼ teaspoon fine sea salt

2 large egg whites, at room temperature

TOPPING

5 ounces semisweet chocolate, finely chopped

1½ teaspoons coconut oil

¼ cup coarsely chopped natural almonds

Position the racks in the top third and center of the oven and preheat the oven to 350°F. Line two large rimmed baking sheets with parchment paper.

To make the macaroons: Mix the coconut, condensed milk, vanilla, and salt together in a large bowl. Whip the egg whites in a small bowl with an electric mixer at high speed just until they form soft peaks. Add the beaten whites to the coconut mixture, and fold the ingredients together.

Using a heaping teaspoon for each, drop the batter onto the prepared baking sheets, spacing the macaroons about 1 inch apart, and using your fingers as needed to help shape them into mounds. Bake, switching the positions of the racks from top to bottom and front to back halfway through baking, until the macaroons are tinged with brown, 15 to 17 minutes. Let them cool on the sheets for 5 minutes. Transfer the macaroons to a wire cooling rack and let cool completely. Set the baking sheets aside to hold the dipped macaroons.

Meanwhile, make the topping: In the top insert of a double boiler over very hot, but not simmering, water (or in a medium heatproof bowl over a medium saucepan), melt the chocolate and coconut oil together, stirring occasionally, being sure that the oil is incorporated into the chocolate. Remove the top insert from the bottom and let the chocolate mixture stand until it has cooled and thickened slightly. If the topping is too hot, it will be too thin to coat the macaroons evenly.

Tilt the insert so the chocolate topping pools on one side. One at a time, dip just the top half of the macaroons into the topping. Return to the baking sheets. While the topping is still liquid, sprinkle the macaroon tops with the almonds. Let the topping cool and set completely, refrigerating the macaroons to speed the setting along, if you wish. (The macaroons can be stored in an airtight container for up to 5 days.)

SNACKS AND BEVERAGES

Here, precooked polenta rounds are lightly pan-fried until crisp and topped with a juicy mushroom sauté as an Italian-inspired warm appetizer. Although we love these as finger food at a casual party, you could also serve them as a vegetarian dinner entrée along with a large salad.

POLENTA "BRUSCHETTA" with MUSHROOMS

MAKES 4 TO 6 SERVINGS

MUSHROOMS

2 tablespoons extra-virgin olive oil

1 pound cremini mushrooms, sliced

Fine sea salt and freshly ground black pepper

2 tablespoons finely chopped shallots

2 teaspoons minced fresh thyme

¼ cup dry white wine

POLENTA ROUNDS

One 18-ounce tube cooked polenta

2 tablespoons extra-virgin olive oil, plus more as needed

Freshly grated Parmigiano-Reggiano cheese, for serving

Finely chopped fresh chives, for serving

To make the mushrooms: Heat the oil in a large skillet over medium-high heat. Add the mushrooms and season them to taste with salt and pepper. Cook, stirring occasionally, until their juices evaporate and the mushrooms are beginning to brown, about 8 minutes. Stir in the shallots and thyme and cook until the shallots soften, about 1 minute. Add the wine and bring to a boil, scraping up the browned bits in the skillet with a wooden spoon. Cook until the wine has evaporated, about 1 minute. Remove the skillet from the heat and cover with the lid ajar to keep the mushrooms warm.

To prepare the polenta rounds: Position a rack in the center of the oven and preheat to 200°F. Cut the polenta into 12 equal rounds. Heat the oil in a large nonstick skillet over medium heat. In batches, add the polenta rounds and cook, flipping them halfway through cooking, until lightly crisped and golden on both sides, and adding more oil as needed, 8 to 10 minutes. Transfer the rounds to a rimmed baking sheet and keep warm in the oven.

To serve, arrange the rounds on a platter. Top each round with a spoonful of the mushrooms, a sprinkle of the Parmigiano, and a scattering of the chives. Serve warm.

Romesco, which hails from Spain, is a zesty spread that doubles as a multipurpose condiment. The Mediterranean flavors of roasted pepper, garlic, and basil go well with just about anything. Try it with grilled fish or spooned over a baked potato.

RED PEPPER and WALNUT ROMESCO

MAKES 1¹/₄ CUPS

2 medium red bell peppers

1 garlic clove, peeled

2 teaspoons balsamic vinegar

2 teaspoons tomato paste

¹/₂ cup coarsely chopped walnuts

¹/₂ cup fresh bread crumbs, made in a blender or food processor from day-old crusty bread

¹/₈ teaspoon red pepper flakes

¹/₄ cup extra-virgin olive oil, as needed

2 tablespoons finely chopped fresh basil

Fine sea salt

Toasted baguette slices or raw vegetables, for serving

Position a rack in the center of the oven and preheat the oven to 450°F.

Place the whole red peppers on a baking sheet. Roast them, turning occasionally, until the skins are deeply browned and blistered, about 40 minutes. (Or, prepare an outdoor grill with medium heat. Cook the peppers on the cooking grate with the lid closed until blackened all over, about 15 minutes.) Transfer the peppers to a heatproof bowl and cover them with a plate. Let stand about 20 minutes. Discard the stem, seeds, and skins from the peppers. Coarsely chop the peppers.

With the machine running, drop the garlic through the feed tube of a food processor to mince the garlic. Add the vinegar and tomato paste, and pulse to dissolve the paste. Add the chopped bell peppers, the walnuts, bread crumbs, and red pepper flakes, and pulse to finely chop the peppers. Add enough of the oil to make a coarse, thick purée. (Or purée the ingredients, including the oil, in batches in a blender.) Transfer to a bowl and stir in the basil. Season to taste with salt. Serve at room temperature with the baguette slices or vegetables for dipping.

RED PEPPERS are a rich source of antioxidants, including vitamins C, A, B6, and E. These help clear the body of free radicals, which can damage cell DNA over time. —MEHMET

With all the commercial crackers out there you may wonder why you should bother to bake your own. Once you taste these crunchy, seeded biscuits, though, you'll know exactly why. Here, I've paired them with marinated feta (page 252), romesco (page 249), and tapenade (page 253), but they're also great for nibbling on their own.

WHOLE WHEAT EVERYTHING CRACKERS

MAKES ABOUT 10½ DOZEN CRACKERS

2 cups unbleached all-purpose flour, plus more for rolling the dough

1 cup whole wheat flour

1 teaspoon granulated garlic or garlic powder

1 teaspoon granulated onion or onion powder

2 teaspoons fine sea salt

¼ cup extra-virgin olive oil

2 teaspoons coarse sea salt, such as Maldon or fleur de sel, or 1 teaspoon kosher salt

1 teaspoon cumin seeds

1 teaspoon nigella seeds or poppy seeds

1 teaspoon flaxseeds

Position the racks in the top third and center of the oven and preheat the oven to 400°F.

Whisk together the all-purpose and whole wheat flours, granulated garlic, granulated onion, and fine salt in a large bowl and make a well in the center. Add the oil and 1 cup water to the well, and stir, adding more water if necessary, to make a stiff dough. Gather up the dough into a ball in the bowl, cover with plastic wrap, and let rest for 10 minutes.

Mix the coarse salt, cumin, nigella, and flaxseeds in a small bowl.

Cut the dough in half. Working with one half at a time, on a lightly floured work surface, roll out the dough into a rough rectangle about ⅛ inch thick. Using a pastry brush, lightly brush the top of the dough with water. Using a pizza wheel or a very sharp knife, cut the dough into pieces measuring about 2 by 3 inches. Sprinkle half of the seed mixture over the dough. Transfer the crackers to large rimmed baking sheets, placing them close together. Repeat with the remaining dough and seed mixture.

Bake, switching the positions of the sheets from top to bottom and front to back halfway through baking, until the crackers are crisp and lightly browned, about 20 minutes. Let cool completely on the baking sheets.

This recipe is extremely simple—so simple that I almost hesitate to call it a recipe. But it's so incredibly delicious that I couldn't in good conscience leave it out. Use the best feta you can find—definitely one packed in brine, and perhaps an imported Greek, French, or Bulgarian variety. If you don't have time to bake the homemade crackers to go with it, pita chips or cut-up veggies will work just fine. Heck, I've been known to eat it right off a spoon.

MARINATED FETA with OREGANO

MAKES ABOUT 2 CUPS

8 ounces fresh feta cheese, drained

2 tablespoons extra-virgin olive oil

1 teaspoon dried oregano

¼ teaspoon red pepper flakes

Whole Wheat Everything Crackers (page 250) or store-bought pita chips, for serving

Place the cheese into a medium bowl. Add the oil, oregano, and red pepper flakes and stir well. Cover the bowl with plastic wrap and let stand at room temperature for 1 to 2 hours. (Or refrigerate for up to 2 days and bring to room temperature before serving.)

Serve with the crackers for spreading.

Tapenade is an all-purpose spread from Provence, with the heady flavors of olives, capers (*tapenas* in Provençale), and garlic. It is traditionally made with anchovies, but I use minced seaweed snacks to provide the same briny flavor.

VEGETARIAN TAPENADE

MAKES 1¼ CUPS

2 garlic cloves, peeled

1 cup pitted black or Kalamata olives

2 tablespoons coarsely chopped fresh flat-leaf parsley

1 tablespoon drained nonpareil capers

1 tablespoon finely chopped seaweed "chips," such as SeaSnax

1 tablespoon coarsely chopped fresh thyme

1 tablespoon fresh lemon juice

¼ teaspoon red pepper flakes

¼ cup extra-virgin olive oil, plus more for storing

Gluten-free crackers or raw vegetables, for serving

With the machine running, drop the garlic through the feed tube of a food processor to mince the garlic. Add the olives, parsley, capers, seaweed, thyme, lemon juice, and red pepper flakes and pulse the mixture until the olives are coarsely chopped. With the machine running, pour the oil through the feed tube to make a coarse purée. (The tapenade can be refrigerated in a covered container, with a thin layer of olive oil poured over the top, for up to 2 weeks. Stir well before using.) Serve the tapenade at room temperature with the crackers or vegetables for dipping.

Anyone who knows Mehmet knows he is crazy about nuts. He likes them raw or soaked, roasted or toasted, and he is rarely found without a baggie full of them tucked away in his pocket. But at home, when he wants something a little more exciting, I bake a tray of these savory snacks. You can use whatever nuts you have in your pantry—this combination just happens to be what is in ours. For a spicier flavor, increase the cayenne slightly, or for a smoky note, substitute ground chipotle.

NOT-TOO-SPICY GLAZED NUTS

MAKES 6 TO 8 SERVINGS

1 tablespoon extra-virgin olive oil

1 tablespoon pure maple syrup

1 garlic clove, minced

1 teaspoon cumin seeds

1 teaspoon nigella seeds

1 teaspoon dried oregano

1/8 teaspoon cayenne pepper

2 1/2 cups unsalted assorted nuts (10 ounces), such as 1/2 cup (2 ounces) each pecan halves, walnut halves, skinned hazelnuts, shelled pistachios, and natural almonds

1/2 teaspoon fine sea salt

Position a rack in the center of the oven and preheat the oven to 350°F.

In a large bowl, mix the oil, maple syrup, garlic, cumin and nigella seeds, oregano, and cayenne. Add the nuts and mix well to coat the nuts. Sprinkle and toss the nuts with the salt. Spread the nuts on a large rimmed baking sheet.

Bake, stirring occasionally to bring the nuts that cook more quickly around the edges into the center, until the nuts are lightly toasted and glazed, about 20 minutes. Let cool on the baking sheet. Break apart the nuts. (The nuts can be stored in an airtight container at room temperature for up to 10 days.)

This snack is salty and sweet with a little kick of heat. The sticky coating clings to the shell so you get plenty of flavor when you pop them in your mouth to extract the bean. Serve these with extra napkins, and expect to have fingers licked at the table.

FINGER-LICKIN' EDAMAME

MAKES 4 SERVINGS

1 pound frozen edamame in the shell

2 tablespoons extra-virgin olive oil

2 tablespoons finely chopped shallots

1 teaspoon peeled and finely shredded fresh ginger (use the small holes on a box grater)

1 garlic clove, minced

¼ teaspoon red pepper flakes

1 tablespoon mirin

1 tablespoon honey

1 teaspoon tamari or soy sauce

1 teaspoon sesame seeds

Fine sea salt

Bring a large saucepan of salted water to a boil over high heat. Add the edamame and boil until the soybeans inside the pods are tender, about 5 minutes. Drain well.

Meanwhile, heat the oil in a large skillet over medium heat. Add the shallots, ginger, and garlic and cook, stirring occasionally, until the shallots are tender, about 2 minutes. Remove from the heat. Stir in the red pepper flakes, followed by the mirin, honey, and tamari. Add the edamame and the sesame seeds and mix well. Season to taste with the salt. Transfer to a serving bowl and serve hot.

It is literally impossible to just have just one bite of these crispy snacks. But go ahead and feel free to binge because these are irresistibly healthy!

CRISPY KALE CHIPS

MAKES 4 TO 6 SERVINGS

1 large bunch kale (about 10 ounces)

3 tablespoons extra-virgin olive oil

2 teaspoons dried oregano

2 garlic cloves, minced

½ teaspoon truffle-flavored salt, plus more to taste

⅛ teaspoon cayenne pepper

¼ cup hemp seeds

Position the racks in the top third and center of the oven and preheat the oven to 300°F.

Strip the thick stems from the kale leaves and discard the stems. Immerse the kale leaves in a sink of cold water and agitate them around to loosen any grit. In batches, lift the kale from the water and spin it dry in a salad spinner. Set the kale aside.

Mix the oil, oregano, garlic, truffle salt, and cayenne together in a large bowl. Add the kale and toss to coat with the oil mixture. Still tossing the kale, sprinkle the leaves with the hemp seeds to coat them as evenly as possible. Divide the kale evenly between two large rimmed baking sheets.

Bake for 20 minutes. Stir the kale and switch the positions of the sheets from top to bottom and front to back. Continue baking until the kale is crisp, about 20 minutes more. (The kale will crisp further when cooled.) Let cool completely. (The kale is best served a few hours after baking.)

HEMP SEEDS have an excellent balance of anti-inflammatory omega-3 and omega-6 fats, which help regulate hormones, improve immune function, and keep skin supple. They are also high in protein. —MEHMET

Sangria is supposed to be Spanish, but our family recipe has a definite Turkish twist. We love the way sweet juices of pomegranate, orange, and melon soften the wine. The mint sprig makes it particularly refreshing on a hot afternoon.

TURKISH SANGRIA with MELON and ORANGE

MAKES 6 TO 8 SERVINGS

One 750-ml bottle fruity red wine, such as merlot or Rioja

¼ cup honey

¼ cup brandy

¼ cup bottled pomegranate juice

1 navel orange, cut into thin half-moons

¼ large ripe crenshaw melon, peeled, seeded, and cut into 1-inch chunks

Fresh mint sprigs, for garnish

Whisk the wine, honey, brandy, and pomegranate juice together in a pitcher to dissolve the honey. Add the orange and melon. Cover the pitcher with plastic wrap and refrigerate to chill and combine the flavors, at least 1 and up to 6 hours.

Pour the sangria into glasses and garnish each with a mint sprig, adding a few ice cubes, if desired. Serve chilled.

I discovered this drink one summer when I was living outside of Paris with a French family who had a daughter my age. She was very chic and very intimidating. One afternoon we went to a café to hang out with her friends, and she ordered this mysterious, vivid red beverage. Seeking to emulate her cool, French *je ne sais quoi*, I ordered the same. Suddenly, I was transformed into an effortlessly stylish woman who could eat entire baguettes and never gain weight. . . . Um, no. But it was fabulous! I made it my signature cocktail when I came home (once I was old enough to order drinks stateside).

MONACO

MAKES 2 SERVINGS

One 12-ounce bottle lager beer

4 tablespoons grenadine

4 tablespoons fresh lime juice

Sparkling water, as needed

2 lime wedges, for garnish

Fill two tall glasses with ice. For each drink, pour in a half bottle of beer, 2 tablespoons of the grenadine, and 2 tablespoons of the lime juice, and stir gently with a long spoon to combine. Top off each with sparkling water to fill the glass and stir again. Garnish with the lime wedge and serve immediately.

Our kids were never allowed to have soft drinks at home, but they sometimes got a little bored with plain old water. As an alternative, I made them big pitchers of these fruit-infused thirst quenchers. They're pretty and fun, and they feel like you're drinking something special (but without added calories or artificial colors and flavoring). Each morning I'd let a different child pick out the flavor of the day. These are our top combinations, but feel free to experiment and come up with some of your own.

CUCUMBER-ORANGE "SPA WATER"

EACH FLAVOR MAKES ABOUT 1 1/2 QUARTS

1 1/2 quarts spring or filtered water

1 navel orange, cut into thin rounds

2 Persian or Israeli cucumbers, cut into thin rounds

Combine the water, orange, and cucumbers in a large pitcher. Use a long wooden spoon to stir and lightly crush the orange and cucumber into the water, releasing their juices and flavors. Let stand for a few minutes for the flavors to combine. Pour into ice-filled glasses and serve.

Lemon-Raspberry: Substitute 1 lemon, cut into thin rounds, and 1⅓ cups fresh raspberries (6 ounces) for the orange and cucumbers.

Strawberry-Pineapple: Substitute 1 cup fresh pineapple chunks and 1 cup thinly sliced strawberries for the orange and cucumbers.

Mango-Lime: Substitute 1 ripe mango, coarsely chopped, and 1 lime, cut into thin rounds, for the orange and cucumbers.

Tangerine-Mint: Substitute 2 tangerines, cut in half crosswise, and 12 large fresh mint sprigs for the orange and cucumbers.

Grapefruit-Thyme: Substitute 1 fresh grapefruit and 12 large fresh thyme sprigs for the orange and cucumbers.

Mehmet loves tequila. On weekends he'll pour himself a shot and sit out on the balcony slowly sipping it while he talks with Oliver about everything from sports to politics. I like tequila, too, but not straight up. I prefer to mix it with a splash of fresh grapefruit juice for a sweetly sour cocktail. The squeeze of ginger juice adds a nice kick.

GINGERED PALOMA

MAKES 2 SERVINGS

1 cup fresh grapefruit juice

6 tablespoons (3 ounces or 2 jiggers) golden tequila

2 tablespoons fresh lime juice

2 tablespoons fresh ginger juice (see Note, page 125)

2 tablespoons agave nectar, preferably dark

Sparkling water, as needed

2 grapefruit wedges, for garnish

Fill two martini glasses with ice. For each drink, pour in ½ cup of the grapefruit juice, 3 tablespoons of the tequila, 1 tablespoon of the lime juice, 1 tablespoon of the ginger juice, and 1 tablespoon of the agave nectar, and stir with a spoon to combine. Top off each with sparkling water to fill the glass and stir again. Garnish with the grapefruit wedge and serve immediately.

This nonalcoholic beverage takes iced tea to a new level with its elegantly perfumed fragrance. Rosewater is a common flavoring in Turkish sweets, and it is available at specialty and Mediterranean grocers. (Be sure to get the culinary rosewater, and not cologne.)

ROSEWATER TEA COOLER

MAKES 2 SERVINGS

3 tea bags black tea, such as English Breakfast

1 navel orange

6 large fresh mint sprigs

2 tablespoons honey

½ teaspoon rosewater

Combine 2 cups water and the tea bags in a small pitcher or jar. Let stand at room temperature until the brewed tea is very strong, about 2 hours. Lift out the tea bags, squeeze the tea from them back into the pitcher, and discard the bags.

Slice two ¼-inch-thick rounds from the center of the orange, and cut the slices into quarters. (Save the remaining orange for another use.) Reserve 2 orange quarters for garnish.

For each drink, add 3 orange quarters, 2 mint sprigs, and 1 tablespoon of the honey to a tall glass. Using a muddler or wooden spoon, crush the orange quarters and mint together. Add ¾ cup of the brewed tea and ¼ teaspoon of rosewater, and stir with a long spoon. Fill the glass with ice. Garnish with the reserved orange quarter and a mint sprig, and serve immediately.

Orange Blossom Tea Cooler: Substitute orange blossom water for the rosewater.

We make a big batch of this delicious fruit and vegetable juice several times a week. It will last for a day or two in the refrigerator, but it's best if you drink it fresh. (The recipe can be halved or doubled based on your family's needs.)

GREEN JUICE

MAKES ABOUT 2 QUARTS

1 pound fresh spinach leaves, stems included, well rinsed

6 celery ribs with leaves

3 large sweet apples, such as Honeycrisp, cut into wedges, but not cored or peeled

2 bunches fresh mint sprigs (about 2 packed cups)

1 bunch fresh flat-leaf parsley (about 1 packed cup)

½ seedless cucumber, unpeeled

½ lime

½ pineapple, peeled and cored, flesh cut into large chunks

6 large carrots

½ lemon

½ navel orange

Using an expeller juicer (either cold-press or centrifugal), juice the ingredients in the order given, pouring the juices into a large bowl. Stir well to combine the juices.

Pour the green juice into large bottles and refrigerate until serving. The juice is best the day it is made.

BASICS

Sautéed chicken is probably the easiest and quickest meat protein to serve as an "add-in" to a grain bowl or salad. Here's a surefire method for cooking it to juicy perfection. One trick is to pound the irregularly shaped breasts to a uniform thickness.

SAUTÉED CHICKEN BREAST

MAKES 4 SERVINGS

2 skinless, boneless chicken breast halves (about 8 ounces each)

1 teaspoon garlic salt

1 teaspoon freshly ground black pepper

1 tablespoon extra-virgin olive oil

One at a time, place the chicken between two large sheets of plastic wrap. Using a flat meat pounder or a rolling pin, lightly pound the chicken until it is an even thickness of about ½ inch. Season the chicken with the garlic salt and pepper.

Heat the oil in a large nonstick skillet over medium-high heat until it is hot but not smoking. Add the chicken and reduce the heat to medium. Cook the chicken until the underside is golden brown, adjusting the heat as necessary so it cooks at an even rate without burning, about 4 minutes. Flip the chicken over and cook until the other side is browned and the chicken feels firm when pressed on top with a fingertip, about 4 minutes more. (Don't bother trying to test for doneness with a meat thermometer, as the probe won't fit properly into this thin cut of chicken, and you'll get an inaccurate reading.) Transfer the chicken to a carving board and let it stand for 3 minutes.

Cut the chicken across the grain into ½-inch strips and serve warm.

Garlic and lemon subtly complement the briny sea flavor of the shrimp without being overpowering, making this another great "add-in" protein for our otherwise vegetarian dishes. Keep a bag of individually frozen shrimp stored in the freezer to bring out on those days when you don't have time to run to the market. They thaw quickly in a big bowl of water, and the "easy peel" variety is a breeze to clean.

QUICK SHRIMP with GARLIC and LEMON

MAKES 4 TO 6 SERVINGS

2 tablespoons extra-virgin olive oil

1 large garlic clove, crushed and peeled

1½ pounds jumbo shrimp (21–25 count), peeled and deveined

Finely grated zest of 1 lemon

2 tablespoons fresh lemon juice

Fine sea salt and freshly ground black pepper

Heat the oil and garlic together in a large skillet over medium heat until tiny bubbles appear around the garlic. Remove and discard the garlic.

Increase the heat to medium-high. Add the shrimp and cook just until they begin to turn opaque around the edges, about 1½ minutes. Flip the shrimp over, and continue cooking just until they are opaque when cut into with the tip of a small knife, about 1½ minutes more. Sprinkle with the lemon zest and juice and stir until the lemon juice evaporates, about 15 seconds. Remove from the heat. Season to taste with the salt and pepper. Transfer the shrimp to a platter. Serve the shrimp warm, cooled, or chilled.

SHRIMP contains carotenoid astaxanthin, an antioxidant that has been shown to protect skin from the sun's ultraviolet rays. Shrimp is also full of omega-3 fatty acids, selenium, and zinc. —MEHMET

There have been quite a few tofu jokes bantered about among certain members of our family. And admittedly, plain tofu can be a bit . . . boring. But soak it in a good marinade and it will take up the flavor brilliantly. Baking tofu gives it a dense texture and earthy taste that even the meat-eaters enjoy.

TERIYAKI BAKED TOFU

MAKES 4 TO 6 SERVINGS

1 tablespoon tamari or soy sauce

1 tablespoon fresh lime juice

1 teaspoon honey

½ teaspoon peeled and finely grated fresh ginger (use the small holes on a box grater)

½ teaspoon toasted sesame oil

¼ cup extra-virgin olive oil

1 pound extra-firm tofu, pressed to remove excess water (see Note, page 50), cut into ¾-inch dice

Whisk the tamari, lime juice, honey, ginger, and sesame oil together in a medium bowl. Gradually whisk in the olive oil. Add the tofu and mix gently to coat with the marinade. Let stand at room temperature for 15 to 45 minutes, the longer the better.

Position a rack in the center of the oven and preheat the oven to 400°F. Lightly oil a rimmed baking sheet.

Spread the tofu with the marinade on the oiled baking sheet, flipping the tofu over halfway through baking, until the tofu is browned, about 30 minutes. Let the tofu cool.

Another quick protein-booster for salads, these turn out slightly crispy and coated with **spices. Make a double batch to store in the refrigerator, as they will keep for a few days.**

SPICED BAKED CHICKPEAS

MAKES 4 TO 6 SERVINGS

One 15-ounce can chickpeas (garbanzo beans), drained, rinsed, and patted dry on paper towels

1 tablespoon extra-virgin olive oil

1 tablespoon fresh lemon juice

1 teaspoon ground cumin

1/2 teaspoon cayenne pepper

Fine sea salt

Position a rack in the center of the oven and preheat the oven to 350°F.

Toss the chickpeas, oil, lemon juice, cumin, and cayenne pepper together in a small bowl. Spread the mixture in a 9 by 13-inch baking dish.

Bake, stirring occasionally, until the chickpeas are lightly browned, 30 to 40 minutes. Season to taste with the salt while the chickpeas are still warm, and let them cool completely. (The chickpeas can be covered and refrigerated for up to 5 days.)

CHICKPEAS (GARBANZO BEANS) have lots of protein and fiber, plus all the building blocks for strong bones, including phosphate and calcium. Chickpeas are also rich in selenium, a mineral that is not present in most fruits and vegetables, and that helps detoxify some cancer-causing compounds in the body. —MEHMET

Some people mistakenly think that farro is an Italian variety of spelt, but it is not, nor is it free of gluten. But it's still a delicious alternative to brown rice, and it cooks more quickly, too. There are usually two kinds of farro sold: whole grain and pearled. Whole-grain farro has the outer coatings of husk and bran intact, which lengthen the cooking time. Pearled farro has had these outer layers removed. Sometimes the type of farro is not indicated, so you may have to be flexible with the cooking time, which runs from about 20 minutes for pearled to 40 minutes for the whole-grain variety.

BASIC FARRO

**MAKES ABOUT
4 1/2 CUPS**

1 1/2 cups pearled farro

1/2 teaspoon fine sea salt

Bring 3 cups water, the farro, and salt to a boil in a medium saucepan over high heat. Cover the saucepan and reduce the heat to medium-low. Simmer until the farro is tender, about 20 minutes. Do not be concerned if some of the cooking water remains. Drain the farro well in a fine-mesh sieve. Serve hot. (The farro can be cooled, covered, and refrigerated for up to 2 days. Or freeze the cooled farro in an airtight plastic bag for up to 3 months; thaw before using.)

FARRO This ancient strain of wheat contains cyanogenic glycosides, which have been shown to help lower cholesterol and boost the immune system. **—MEHMET**

Our family loves brown rice. It has a warm, nutty flavor and is loaded with B vitamins and fiber. But its approximate cooking time of almost an hour can be a bit daunting, especially on a weeknight. The solution is to cook the rice when you have time and freeze it for a future meal. I prefer the short-grain variety, but use whatever you like.

BASIC BROWN RICE

MAKES ABOUT 6 CUPS

2 cups long-grain brown rice

1 teaspoon fine sea salt

Bring 4 cups water, the rice, and salt to a boil in a large saucepan over high heat. Reduce the heat to low and cover. Simmer until the rice is tender and has absorbed the water, about 45 minutes. Remove the rice from the heat and let stand for 5 minutes. Fluff the rice with a fork. Serve hot. (The rice can be cooled, covered, and refrigerated for up to 2 days. Or freeze the cooled rice in an airtight plastic bag for up to 3 months; thaw before using.)

BROWN RICE I have always enjoyed the richness of brown rice more than white versions, but the health benefits are immense as well. Brown rice is produced by only removing the outermost layer of the rice kernel, which does not create a nutritional penalty. The complete milling and polishing that converts brown rice into white rice removes most of the vitamins B_1, B_3, and B_6, as well as half of the manganese and phosphorus. Plus, you lose the dietary fiber and essential fatty acids, so the decision should be easy. —MEHMET

BASIC COOKED BEANS

It is difficult to beat the convenience of canned beans, and our pantry is filled with a large variety, with black, cannellini (white kidney), and chickpeas (garbanzo beans) leading the pack. That being said, when I have the time, I prefer to soak and boil them myself. Here are some tips on cooking dried beans:

- Dried beans do have a shelf life of about six months after purchase. Buy them at a reliable store with a steady turnover, as old beans take forever to cook. If you are only cooking part of a bag, store the leftover dried beans at room temperature in an airtight container, such as a jar.

- Always sort through the dried beans before cooking for any stones or bits of dirt. Rinse the beans well under cold running water and drain them before soaking or cooking.

- Soaking the dried beans helps to hydrate them so they cook more evenly and quickly. The jury is out on whether soaking weakens the complex sugars that cause digestion problems.

- It is a myth that beans need to soak overnight. Two to 3 hours is enough for small beans (such as adzuki or black), and the larger beans (white kidney and chickpeas) won't soak up much more water after 4 hours. Lentils are a favorite because they don't have to be soaked at all, so they supply almost instant gratification.

- There are two methods for soaking beans (or skip the soaking and extend the estimated cooking time by about one-third). For standard soaking, put the rinsed beans in a large bowl and add enough cold water to cover them by at least 2 inches. Soak at cool room temperature for 2 to 4 hours, depending on the size of the bean. For the quick-soak method, put the rinsed beans in a large saucepan and add enough water to cover them by 2 inches. Bring to a boil over high heat and cook for 1 minute. Remove the saucepan from the heat and cover it tightly. Let the beans stand in the water for 1 hour. With both methods, drain the beans well.

· To cook 1 cup (8 ounces) beans after soaking, put them in a large saucepan, and add enough cold, salted water to cover them by 2 inches. (How much salt? Just taste it, and if you can detect the salt, but it doesn't taste like ocean water, you have enough.) Bring the beans to a boil over high heat. Reduce the heat to low. Simmer, uncovered, until the beans are cooked, using the list below as a guide. You always have to allow some leeway for the cooking time, based on the age and relative dryness of the beans.

APPROXIMATE COOKING TIMES FOR DRIED BEANS

Most beans are soaked and drained before cooking. One cup (8 ounces) of dried beans yields about 3 cups cooked beans.

BLACK (TURTLE): 60 to 90 minutes

BLACK-EYED PEAS (DO NOT SOAK): 45 to 60 minutes

CANNELLINI (WHITE KIDNEY): 45 to 60 minutes

CHICKPEAS (GARBANZO): 60 to 75 minutes

CRANBERRY: 45 to 60 minutes

GREAT NORTHERN: 45 to 60 minutes

LENTILS (DO NOT SOAK): 30 to 45 minutes

LIMAS (BABY): 45 to 60 minutes

NAVY: 45 to 60 minutes

PINK: 45 to 60 minutes

PINTO: 60 to 75 minutes

RED: 60 to 75 minutes

RED KIDNEY: 60 to 75 minutes

There are times when a tasty cooking broth will add oomph to certain dishes. For those occasions, I recommend having a reserve of this broth stored in the freezer. It's more than just the usual suspects simmered together; a big potato gives it a rich consistency and dried mushrooms contribute an umami depth of flavor.

ALL-PURPOSE VEGETABLE BROTH

MAKES ABOUT 2 1/2 QUARTS

2 tablespoons extra-virgin olive oil

1 large yellow onion, coarsely chopped

2 medium carrots, coarsely chopped

2 medium celery ribs with leaves, coarsely chopped

1 large baking potato, scrubbed, cut into 1-inch chunks

1 cup (1 ounce) loosely packed dried mushrooms, preferably porcini, quickly rinsed

1 head garlic, unpeeled, cut in half crosswise

6 sprigs fresh flat-leaf parsley

4 sprigs fresh thyme, or 1/2 teaspoon dried thyme

1/2 teaspoon black peppercorns

1 large dried bay leaf

Heat the oil in a large pot over medium heat. Add the onion, carrots, and celery. Cook, stirring occasionally, until the onion is golden but not browned, about 5 minutes.

Add 3 quarts water, the potato, dried mushrooms, garlic, parsley, thyme, peppercorns, and bay leaf and bring to a boil over high heat. Reduce the heat to low and simmer until the stock is slightly reduced, full flavored, and the potato is falling apart, about 1½ hours.

Strain the broth through a fine-mesh sieve or colander into a very large bowl. Discard the solids in the sieve. (The broth can be cooled, covered, and refrigerated for up to 5 days. Or store the cooled broth in freezer-safe containers for up to 3 months.)

This is our customary marinade for all types of vegetables. We like to just lightly coat the vegetables with it before grilling, but feel free to double the recipe if you prefer to drench the veggies.

VEGETABLE MARINADE

**MAKES ABOUT
1/2 CUP**

2 tablespoons balsamic vinegar

1 teaspoon dried oregano

1 garlic clove, crushed through a garlic press

1/2 teaspoon fine sea salt

1/4 teaspoon red pepper flakes

1/3 cup extra-virgin olive oil

Whisk the vinegar, oregano, garlic, salt, and red pepper flakes together in a small bowl. Gradually whisk in the oil.

Puréed avocado gives this dressing a thickness that is especially good with sturdy greens like romaine. In fact, it's rich enough to serve as a dip for raw vegetables. Make the dressing in a food processor or blender so the ingredients are really well combined.

CREAMY AVOCADO SALAD DRESSING

**MAKES ABOUT
1 CUP**

⅓ cup extra-virgin olive oil

½ ripe Hass avocado, coarsely chopped

2 tablespoons red wine vinegar

1 tablespoon fresh lemon juice

1 tablespoon minced shallot

1 tablespoon minced fresh chives

1 teaspoon Dijon mustard

½ teaspoon tamari or soy sauce

1 teaspoon pure maple syrup

Fine sea salt and freshly ground black pepper

Add the oil, avocado, vinegar, lemon juice, shallot, chives, mustard, tamari, and maple syrup to a food processor or blender and process until smooth. Season to taste with salt and pepper.

Every household needs a go-to vinaigrette for everyday meals. I love this one because it touches all the bases. Dijon mustard gives the dressing a bit of spice and helps thicken it, too. I adore fresh chives, so I always have some on hand, but you could substitute a tablespoon or so of minced scallion tops or shallot, if preferred.

OZ FAMILY HOUSE DRESSING

**MAKES ABOUT
1 CUP**

1 teaspoon Dijon mustard

1 garlic clove, crushed through a garlic press

3 tablespoons cider vinegar

1 teaspoon pure maple syrup

1/2 teaspoon tamari or soy sauce

1/4 teaspoon fine sea salt

1/4 teaspoon freshly ground black pepper

2/3 cup extra-virgin olive oil

1 tablespoon finely chopped fresh chives

Whisk the mustard and garlic together in a small bowl. Add the vinegar, maple syrup, tamari, salt, and pepper and whisk well. Gradually whisk in the oil. (Or combine all of the ingredients in a jar and shake well.) Stir in the chives. (The dressing can be covered and refrigerated for up to 3 days. Whisk well before using.)

VINEGAR is a powerful antimicrobial and is full of polyphenols that help mitigate oxidative stress. Vinegar helps stabilize blood sugar by slowing the absorption of carbohydrates, and may aid in weight loss by increasing satiety. —MEHMET

ACKNOWLEDGMENTS

While I always think of writing as a solitary craft, publishing a book is downright social—a cookbook, even more so. With that in mind there are a number of people I would like to thank:

I am forever indebted to our children, Daphne, her husband John, Arabella, Zoe, and Oliver. This is really their book, too.

Next I need to thank my mother, Emily Jane, for teaching me pretty much all I know about food. Thanks also to my father, Gerald Michael, for passing down the secret Gypsy recipes.

Thank you to my siblings, Laura, Emily, Michael, Samantha, and Christopher for being my favorite kitchen companions over the years.

My soul sister, Susan Novick, has been a constant source of support and encouragement and a steadfast supplier of tea during the procrastination, I mean, writing phase of this book.

My personal cheerleading team, Michelle Bouchard, Joel Harper, Alicia Haywood, Barbara Grimaldi—thank you all for believing in me even when I'm not so sure myself.

My brilliant agent and dear friend, Jennifer Walsh, is my guardian angel. This book was a gift from her to me.

I'd like to thank my former editor, Dominick Anfuso, without whom I would have no writing career. He envisioned this book before I did.

And many thanks to my current editor, Diana Baroni. Her patience and wise guidance were invaluable throughout the entire process.

The team at Harmony Books/Crown Publishing is incredible. Marysarah Quinn, Stephanie Huntwork, Christine Tanigawa, Michele Eniclerico, Tammy Blake, Julie Cepler—you guys are the best in the business! An extra shout-out to my fabulous art director, Michael Nagin, who not only has a great eye, but also knows all the hottest places to eat in NYC.

Rick Rodgers started as a recipe tester but quickly became my culinary mentor and kitchen confidant. His generosity both personally and professionally is extraordinary. This book would have been impossible without him.

Thank you to my spectacular photographer, Quentin Bacon. He has a remarkable talent for making the mundane beautiful—and he's got the most awesome accent this side of Melbourne. I liked hanging out in the studio just to listen to him speak.

Giant thank-yous to his wonderful team: Maya Rossi, magnificent prop stylist and gentle soul; Suzanne Lenzer, miracle-working food stylist, who, along with Kate Schmidt and Erica Clark, cooks food that actually looks as good as it tastes; Kristen Walther, an absolute genius with a computer and hands down the coolest girl in the room.

Thank you to Kara Lowery, my lovely hair stylist and makeup artist who was unfazed by having to beautify our whole family.

Thank you to my amazing team at *Dr. Oz The Good Life*. And a special thanks to Ellen Levine, Jill Herzig, and Bruce Perez for their expert guidance with this project.

Donna O'Sullivan, I literally could not function without you. Thank you for being my genie in a bottle (each day is another three wishes) and my friend.

Aleida Valcarcel, Turgut and Necmiye Kacaroglu, and Mike Wujek—thank you for taking care of the important things and for tasting all the recipes in this book (and the ones that didn't make the cut).

Finally and most of all, I'd like to thank my husband, Mehmet—for everything.

INDEX